A History of Alston Moor

by

Alastair Robertson

2nd Enlarged Edition

Hundy Publications
2010

First published 1998
2nd print 1999
3rd print 2002
2nd Enlarged Edition 2010

Hundy Publications, Ashleigh House, Alston, Cumbria CA9 3SN

CONTENTS

LIST OF ILLUSTRATIONS

All illustrations are from the Alston Moor Historical Society except where stated.

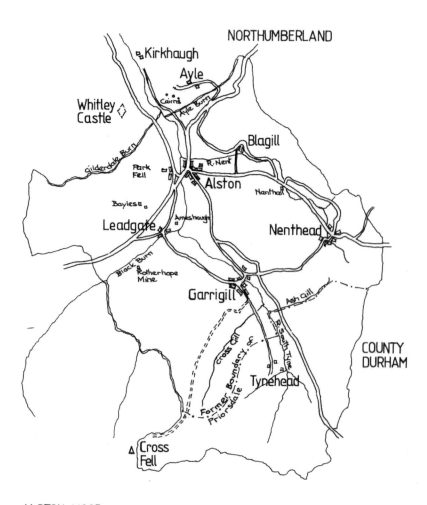

ALSTON MOOR

NORTHUMBERLAND

Kirkhaugh

Ayle

Cairns

Ayle Burn

Whitley
Castle

Gilderdale Burn

Blagill

R. Nent

Park
Fell

Alston

Nenthall

Bayles

Ameshaugh

Leadgate

Nenthead

Black Burn

Rotherhope
Mine

Garrigill

Ash Gill

Cross Gill

R. South Tyne

Former Boundary of
Priorsdale

COUNTY
DURHAM

Tynehead

Cross
Fell

INTRODUCTION

Alston Moor lies just below the line of latitude 55 degrees north and is 2½ degrees west of Greenwich. In area it covers between 70 and 80 square miles. The altitude ranges from 800ft (250m) above sea level at Randleholme on the county boundary with Northumberland, to 2,930ft (893m) at the peak of Cross Fell. Geologically, the Moor forms a part of and gives its name to the Alston Block, which is an almost rectangular slab of rock separated from its neighbouring formations by faults on three sides. The Block stretches from the Tyne Gap in the north to the Stainmore Pass in the south and gently tilts from the western Pennine scarp of Cross Fell down to the coast of County Durham in the east.

Throughout its recorded history, Alston Moor has been exploited for its mineral wealth, mainly for the lead, for which it is famous, and silver extracted from the lead, but iron ore, zinc, copper, limestone, sandstone, whinstone, fluorspar, umber and coal have also been worked.

The main thoroughfare in the town of Alston climbs from 886ft (270m) at the Nent Bridge to 1084ft (320m) on the Nenthead Road in the space of 800 yards - Front Street is good training for hill walkers.

The Market Square in Alston

Alston claims to be the highest market town in England but it is many years since a market was last held. Nenthead and Garrigill, incidentally, clock in at 1450ft (438m) and 1125ft (340m) above sea level respectively.

In 1811 a trades directory described the buildings of Alston as "rather mean and disagreeable". Nowadays the town is regarded as quaint, attractive, relatively unspoiled and a suitable location for TV dramatisations of such stories as 'Jane Eyre', 'Oliver Twist' and Catherine Cookson's novels.

It is twelve years since the first edition of 'A History of Alston Moor' was published, followed by two reprints, the last one in 2002, so it is time for a new, expanded edition. But even with extra material, this book can still only be a whistle-stop historical tour of Alston Moor, with occasional detailed forays into subjects that have taken my fancy.

Alastair Robertson
October 2010

FROM PREHISTORIC TIMES TO 1700

Before the Romans

Until very recently, our knowledge of prehistoric times relied on a few stray finds and only one 'dig', but the English Heritage 'Miner-Farmer' project currently under way in 2010 has revealed a large amount of human activity.

When the first edition of 'A History of Alston Moor' was published in 1998, the only known traces of early human habitation in the area were two small Bronze Age burial mounds at Kirkhaugh and 'lumps and bumps' in a field at Banks Farm near Alston. Now, aerial photography and 'Lidar' computer images are revealing many pre-Roman settlements all over the Moor, as well as a possible 'henge'. Two of the settlements are of particular interest; they lie very close to the Roman fort of Whitley Castle and demonstrate occupation before, during, and possibly after the Romans came and went. A well-defined settlement can be seen at Banks Farm, on the south facing valley-side of the River Nent, where there are prehistoric cultivation terraces, trackways and the outlines of a cluster of buildings nearby.

When the Kirkhaugh mounds were excavated in 1935 they were dated to between 2,000BC and 1,700BC. One contained the remains of an unburnt burial, broken pottery, a flint arrowhead and flint and stone tools. It also contained a gold earring which possibly came from Spain; this is very rare and famous in its own way, known as 'the Kirkhaugh earring'. The other barrow held only an empty burial cist. It had evidently been opened at some time, for the sole remaining artefact was a broken stone rubbing tool.

There are also a few stray finds of artifacts on record. William Wallace, a local historian and lead mining authority of the late nineteenth century, owned a polished stone hatchet that had been found two or three feet below the surface of an ancient landslip west of Nenthead. At the Raise housing estate near

The Kirkhaugh gold earring

4

Alston a small flint knife was found in one of the gardens when it was newly dug in 1966, a piece of worked flint was found in a field near the Brewery in 1916, a broken mid-Bronze Age axe was found "in the Alston district", and 19cm long spearhead was found at Ashgill.

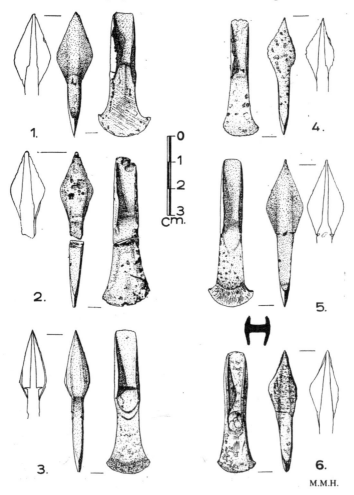

Fig. 1. 1, Ewart Park, Wooler; 2, Alston District; 3, Chollerton; 4, Halton Chesters; 5, Branshaw, Elsdon; 6, Eastnook, Elsdon

M.M.H.

Bronze Age axes, including one found at Alston

The native British, otherwise Celts, left their legacy in the form of place names, relating to Welsh Gaelic rather than Scots Gaelic. The River Nent is the same as the modern Welsh 'nant' which means valley or stream. The Tyne is a Celtic river name from the word 'ti' or 'tei', meaning to dissolve, to flow. There is also the local place name of Hundy, which could well be derived from the Welsh 'hwnt', meaning 'yonder', and 'daea', meaning 'land'. 'Yonder land' is an apt description of Alston Moor from any direction. Near Garrigill is the oldest named lead mine on Alston Moor, 'Fletcher's'. In olden times this was 'Fleccheroos', which could come from the Celtic 'rhos', meaning 'moor'.

Roman Occupation

When the Romans arrived on Alston Moor, it was not to an empty landscape, the area had a well established native population that appears to have co-existed with the Romans. Their settlements are still quite visible - if you know what to look for. The fort at Whitley Castle, two miles north of Alston, may have been an army camp in the early second century, but it was certainly a fort from the mid-2nd century to the late 4th century that served as a halfway stop on the Maiden Way, the road from Kirby Thore in the Eden valley to Greenhead in the Tyne valley. But its main purpose was to control and safeguard the lead and silver extraction from the upper reaches of the South Tyne valley.

The Roman name for Whitley Castle is probably Epiacum, meaning the estate of Eppius, a Romanised British name, and Epiacum was one of the nine Brigantian towns listed by the geographer Ptolemy. The fort lies on a shelf of land protruding from the valley side, commanding views all around except to the west side, here the complex of defensive ramparts is one of the two best preserved examples in the whole Roman Empire. The evidence from a small trench dig in the 1950's, and records of occasional finds of altars and inscribed stones, most of which have vanished, indicated that the fort was destroyed at least once and rebuilt on two occasions. The Sixth and Twentieth legions took part in the construction work and it was garrisoned during the third century by the Second Cohort of Nervians, who came from the Lower Rhine. The adjacent civilian settlement can be seen on aerial photographs as a mesh of intersecting straight lines. That women and children lived there was shown by finds of shoes in a midden discovered by chance in the 1820's.

Whitley Castle near Alston viewed from the north west.

At Tynehead, some eight miles south of Alston, is a field which used to be known as 'Chesters'. Here is evidence of shallow pits that were worked for alluvial lead ore and its by-product of silver. Lead package seals from metal works of the Nervians from Alston Moor were found at the fort of Brough. The earthwork of Hall Hill, believed to be a Roman site, overlooks the confluence of the rivers South Tyne and Nent at Alston. Two Roman bronze measuring jugs were found there in 1839.

The 'Dark Ages'

The Romans left the area around 367AD, to be followed by Anglo-Saxon and later Viking invaders and settlers who mixed with the resident Celtic population. As with the Celts, place names show their presence on the Moor. The most prominent Saxon place name is 'shield', for example Newshield, Lovelady Shield and Foreshield, which was the name given to the huts lived in during the upland summer grazing of the flocks and herds. This word is similar in meaning to the Norse 'skalis', as in 'Scalebank'.

'Byr', a farm or an estate, was used in 'Low Byre'. The Viking 'fjall' became 'fell'. 'Fors', a waterfall, became 'force' which, for example, combined with the Celtic 'Nent' to become Nent Force. 'Crook' came from 'krokr', meaning a bend or crook, as in Crookbank and Crookburn. 'Gil', a dene or glen, is to be found all over. Garrigill uses the Saxon forename 'Gerard', to make what was, in olden days, Gerardsgile; 'Nattrass' which, as well as being a surname, could come from 'nata', meaning 'nettle'; Galligill may derive from 'galgi', meaning 'gallows'; and Skydes from the plural of 'skid', a billet of wood. The town of Alston has been spelt Aldstone, Aldenby and Aldenstone, and could mean the Saxon Aldwin's tun, or town.

Above Banks Farm near Alston is a ruined steading called Four Dargue. The word is pronounced "darg" and comes from the Anglo-Saxon 'doeg-weorc', meaning a day's work. At times it could be the day of work that was due to the lord of the manor by his tenants and be referred to as a 'boon dargue'. In another sense it was the area of land that could be ploughed in a day, but in the north Pennines where there is very little arable farming, the meaning of the word dargue would be the area of land that could be mown in a day.

The local lead mine agent and author William Wallace observed that the Saxon settlers built a turf dyke and ditch in the valley bottoms to prevent cattle from straying from the uplands onto the low lying land during the summer months in order to allow hay to grow there for winter fodder. The dyke and ditch could have formed early tenement or estate boundaries and might be the 'dyke' mentioned in the Drift Roll, an important document of local land administration written before 1500.

Before the arrival of the Normans, Alston Moor was affiliated more to the old kingdom of Northumbria and later in the earldom of Northumberland. Then in the twelfth century, for twenty years or so during the anarchy between King Stephen and Empress Maud, it was part of Scotland under King David (1124–1153) before it became part of the Liberty of Tynedale, one of the Scottish king's estates in England.

In 1152 Henry, Archbishop of York, complained to King David that the lead miners were ravaging the forests. One of the miners' privileges was the right to cut down any trees they chose for their own needs.

The north of England before 1070

The Liberty of Tynedale encompassed an area from the present day Scottish border, down the North and South Tyne valleys as far south as Cross Fell on Alston Moor and as part of the Scottish king's estates in England it was administratively separate in many ways from its neighbouring counties. This situation led to centuries of doubt about the status of Alston Moor. For instance, as late as the end of the thirteenth century, in his wars against the Scots, Edward I ordered an assessment of the boundaries of Cumberland as it has been at its partition in 1070 to help clarify the situation. Alston Moor was not included.

Alston Moor in the Middle Ages

The de Veteriponts

In 1092, King William II came north with a large army, drove out Dolphin, Lord of Cumberland, from Carlisle and established an English colony there. He rebuilt the city and firmly took Cumberland for the English crown. The lead mine on Alston Moor was already known to have a high silver content suitable for coining and, because of the newly established royal mint in Carlisle, the area soon afterwards became permanently linked with Cumberland.

The earliest evidence for Norman lead mining on Alston Moor was reputedly found in the mid-nineteenth century when a lead miner named Joseph Winskill re-opened an old drift on the Browngill vein near Garrigill. In doing so he found coins which he took to the vicar of Alston, the Rev. Hugh Salvin, who identified them as being from the reign of William II (1087-1100).

The oldest document referring to Alston Moor is from the reign of Henry I (1100-1135). The Pipe Roll, the document of royal revenues, for the year 1130-1131 notes the rental of the silver mine of Carlisle that later references show to be on Alston Moor, the only silver mine of that time.

The de Veteripont family appeared on Alston Moor in the middle of the twelfth century. They were first recorded as lords of the manor of Langton in the Tweed valley near Berwick, before also becoming lords of the manor of Alston Moor, holding it on behalf of the kings of Scotland from the kings of England as part of the Liberty of Tynedale.

The kings of England retained the mineral rights in Tynedale and because of this the administration of Alston Moor was not straightforward. The majority of people in the area were tenants of the Scottish king, whereas the miners were subject directly to the English king with separate rights and privileges, and the de Veteriponts administered them both. This divided sovereignty was clearly open to abuse and the de Veteriponts acted in an independent manner.

William de Veteripont was the first Lord of the Manor of Alston Moor. He married Maud de Morville, who held land in the Eden valley and by her he had two sons, Ivo and Robert. Robert, the younger son, through his own efforts and subsequent favour with King John, became Lord of Appleby, Sheriff of Cumberland and Westmorland, and ancestor of the Clifford family.

Ivo, as the eldest son, inherited the estate and lordship of Alston Moor, as well as Mauld's Meaburn, Blencarn and Ainstable in the Eden valley, Elrington and Kirkhaugh in Northumberland, and Ireby and Waverton to the west of Carlisle. For some time he held the custody of Mount Sorrel Castle in Leicestershire, which he lost in King John's war with the barons in 1216.

On 10th May 1209, while King John was inspecting the construction of the Augustinian Priory at Hexham on a visit to the north, he confirmed the Lordship of Alston Moor to Ivo. In return, Ivo made a very generous gift to the new priory of all his demesne land at Alston, to be held of him and his heirs "in perpetual alms". There was "common pasture for 40 cows, 10 mares and 100 sheep, with their respective followers until two years old", also other land on both sides of the Tyne above the bridge at Alston as far as the Nattrass Gill, with liberty to grind corn grown on the same lands at the mill of Alston, "without giving multure", the toll paid to a miller.

In addition, Ivo gave the prior and canons 2,000 acres of moor and pasture at what became known as Priorsdale at Tynehead, with the following notice to the rest of the inhabitants of Alston Moor:

> *"They have also free ingress, transit, and exit, throughout the whole fee of Alston, to the aforesaid Presdale, without hindrance on the part of anyone, and also for men of the aforesaid Prior and Convent, and for their animals of every kind; neither shall they be challenged (let them be) or disturbed, whether going or coming (returning or crossing) by causing delay, by day or night, in the pasture of Alston, with their cattle; outside the divisions of Presdale first named. And the aforesaid Prior and (members of) the convent have the right of communication through all the pasture of Alston-moor, with all their animals going out of Presdale, every day, just as they please, from sun rise to sun set, without any interference whatsoever."*

The extent of Priorsdale covered about one third of Alston Moor, described in 'The Black Book' of Hexham Priory, a rent roll from the thirteenth century but still valid at the time of the dissolution of the monasteries in 1539.

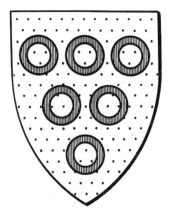

The de Veteripont Arms

The lead mine

During the twelfth century *"the lead mine of Carlisle"* was on Alston Moor, referred to in the singular, and it was very productive. In 1167 lead from the mine was being taken to *"the king's houses at Windsor"*, and in 1177, *"100 cartloads of lead (were) delivered to brother Simon to the work of the church of Clarevall"*, the Cistercian abbey at Clairvaux in Normandy near the present border with Germany.

During the reign of Henry II (1154-1189), William, son of Erembald, rented 'the silver mine' in 1158 for 100 silver marks (£66.13s.4d.) and in 1159 for £100. It must have been very profitable for the rent escalated further, reaching 500 marks (£333.13s.4d.) a year by 1166. However, the boom ceased and by 1179 the debt of unpaid rent owed by William was a colossal £2,000. This debt lingered for at least another thirty-five years, with no attempt by the Crown to retrieve it. After a time the mine decreased in value and by 1211 it was rented out at just 10 marks (£6.13s.4d.) per year.

The rent for the mine was temporarily reduced further in 1222 to five marks per annum because it was not being worked at all, but in 1223 the full rent of ten marks was reinstated, together with every ninth disc of ore dug up. (A disc was as much lead as a strong man could lift from the ground.) The miners were also given letters of protection of their status until the young king, Henry III (1216-1272), came of age.

In 1225 complaints were being made to King Henry's guardian that Ivo de Veteripont, Lord of the Manor, was ill-treating the miners and imprisoning them, yet in that same year, on assurances of security, Ivo was appointed collector of the king's mine taxes.

In 1234 Henry took all miners and their goods under his protection for an extra payment by them of five marks, and the next year he ordered all his miners in Cumberland to come and work on Alston Moor. In return they were to receive all rights and privileges, they would be guaranteed safety and security, and, because it was such an isolated part of the world, they would be supplied with victuals. In 1237, Henry again granted them protection for a fee of twenty shillings and endorsed their privileges, with a £10 fine for anyone who molested them.

The church

The first record of a church on Alston Moor was in 1154 and it is possible that the Chapelry of Garrigill was established at the same time, it was certainly in existence in 1215.

The church of St. Augustine of Canterbury in Alston is situated very prominently on a shelf of land overlooking the valley. If this is the site of the original Norman, or even Anglo-Saxon, church, it would have been obvious to all to see, emphasising the church's presence in the area.

Three gravestones survive in St. Augustine's Church from this early period. The emblems they show are, a pair of shears, the emblem of a woman (the equivalent of kitchen scissors a mediaeval housewife would wear on her girdle), another, larger slab also dedicated to a woman, but carved alongside the shears is a cross-like symbol.

Small slabs such as these, bearing only an emblem (usually the sword for men or shears for women), usually have a 12th or 13th century date. Besides these, there are two fragments of a large grave cover, that of a cleric.

Who these people were that were important enough to merit gravestones we can never know, but we can at least take a guess at the identity of the priest. The clues are, 1) an important cleric, and, 2) buried in the late 12th or 13th century.

Alston Moor in the later 12th century was part of the estate of the kings of Scotland and at the same time it was a valuable asset to the kings of England who held the mineral rights. The lead mine here was providing silver for the royal mint at Carlisle, lead was transported for use at Windsor Castle and exported to France, and the rent of the mine was a valuable asset. A place such as Alston would deserve some symbol of its high status.

Henry II had retained for the kings of England the advowson, or right of patronage, of the church here, and one of the first acts that he carried out on his accession to the throne in 1154, was to personally nominate a priest, whose name was Galfrid, to the church at Alston.

Supposing that on his appointment Galfrid was a youngish man who lived here until his death in old age, about 1200, then, from the date of the grave slab, it could have been his. He was certainly a priest of high status, appointed by the king himself, and as such he would have warranted this ornate gravestone.

In 1232 Ivo's gift of Priorsdale to the Priors of Hexham was confirmed by King John's son and successor, Henry III. By this time, since the decline in importance of the lead mines, the priors had acquired the advowson to the churches at Alston and Garrigill.

But in 1291 Edward I overruled the Prior of Hexham's claim to present the vicar of Alston and claimed the greater right to present his own choice, Hugh, son of Elias Brengewenne, to the church at Alston, which he did on 30th December 1292. Also in 1291 the 'Valor Ecclesiasticus' of Pope Nicholas IV showed the church of Alston to be in the diocese of Durham, where it remained until combined with other diocese into the newly-created Bishopric of Newcastle in 1882.

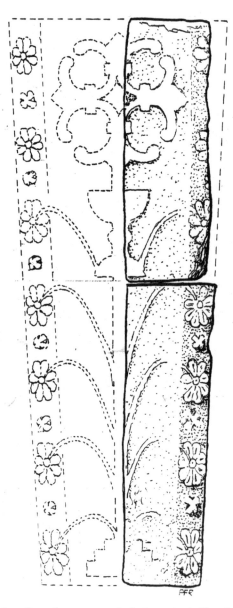

A mediaeval grave stone in St Augustine's Church

15

Edward then changed his mind and in 1299 the church and its advowson were given to Hexham Priory. But in 1306, during the 34th year of his reign when he was lying ill at Lanercost Priory near Brampton, although Edward confirmed the advowson to the Priory, he kept the church itself for the Crown. This situation lasted until 1378, when, during the reign of Richard II, Hexham Priory appropriated Alston's church.

A thirteenth century bronze skillet found at Alston

Politics and mining

The former Roman fort of Whitley Castle, which became the manor of Whitlaw, was still a place of some significance. In 1222 the sheriff of Northumberland, the bishop of Durham or his bailiff, three barons and other loyal knights stopped there to determine the borders of the Marches between England and Scotland. In 1906 a thirteenth century bronze skillet was unearthed near the fort by a farmer digging turf to repair a boundary. The designs upon it of a dragon and scroll work are rare in metal objects and of high quality. It would have belonged to a person of high rank or else it was made for a specific, very important purpose. Had one of the cooks for the noble party left this utensil behind?

Ivo de Veteripont died in 1239 and the lordship passed to his eldest son, Robert who died childless and the title then passed to the next brother in line, Nicholas. Nicholas began to deprive the miners of their rights and in 1246 they petitioned the king to hold assizes at Aimshaugh, but there is no record that this hearing took place.

During the thirteenth century the lead mines were not profitable and the miners must have been practically redundant and so were made available to work for the Scottish king, for on the 7th September 1255 Henry III wrote,

> *"The King to the Sheriff of Cumberland. Directs him to pay the King's miners of Aldeston who came to the King of Scotland, by his precept, 20s. for their labours and expenses incurred in coming to Werk".*

The village of Wark in the North Tyne valley was the Scottish king's administrative centre for the Liberty of Tynedale.

Edward I (1272-1307) decided to revive the English royal interest. In 1278 he reclaimed the Manor from Nicholas's son, Robert, after a series of assizes over complaints about Robert appropriating the mines from the king and running them in his own interests. This alienation had been initiated years before by his grandfather Ivo's manorial tenant, Ranulf de Levington. Robert was also accused of a string of other offences, including harbouring felons, of obstructing *"a useful road leading from Alston to Gossipgate"*, of obstructing the English king's bailiffs in their duty, of not taking up a knighthood, even though he possessed lands to the value of a knight's fee, and of moving the king's gallows from Aimshaugh to Bayles.

Robert was called upon to prove his title, which he did successfully after the involvement of Prince Alexander, the son of King Alexander III of Scotland, who was himself questioned as to his rights as tenant-in-chief to Alston Moor. King Alexander himself had been to London to do homage to Edward for the lands he held in England.

On 21st June 1279, Edward returned the Manor of Alston Moor to Alexander III when, at the same time, it was found to be indisputably a part of Cumberland. The Moor was referred to, however, as being in the

17

Marches of Scotland. The lordship without the mines was then restored to Robert's son, Nicholas, in 1282, Robert having died in the meantime.

When the hearing of 1279 confirmed that the kings of Scotland held Alston Moor and acknowledged that the kings of England owned the mines beneath, the miners who worked them were distinct from the rest of the community and paid their dues of ten marks for their liberties to the king of England, not to the Scottish king. The miners were a law unto themselves. They lived in separate, self-regulating communities under royal protection. They elected their own spokesmen, one as a Coroner and one as a King's Sergeant to administer and execute their own laws. It was only much later in 1426, when the Stapleton family, who already held the franchise of the mines, inherited the lordship of the manor, that the miners became integrated with the rest of society and their independence ceased.

The north of England before 1296

The earliest reference to a possible site for lead smelting was at the assizes of 1279, when the Robert de Veteripont was accused of moving the king's gallows from Aimshaugh to Bayles. The clue is in the word 'bayle'. A 'bayle', or sometimes 'bole', was an early form of furnace. There are houses in the district named Middle Bayles and High Bayles, to the west of the A686 Penrith road about a mile south west from Alston, and another Bayle Hill at the top of Potters Loaning just to the south of Alston.

Part of Park Fell, the hill above Bayles, according to the Drift Roll of the reign of Henry VII (a document setting out rights of way for driving livestock onto the fells), was known as 'haggs', a name associated with peat extraction that was fuel for early smelters as well as trees.

In obtaining trees for fuel the miners on at least one occasion exceeded their rights. In 1290 Henry and Joan de Whitley (usually incorrectly referred to as Whitby) indicted Patric-of-the-Gile and twenty-six other miners who, by force of arms, felled more than their rightful share of trees on their land, to the value of £40.

Boundary Crosses

The restoration of Alston Moor to the king of Scotland in 1279 and his tenant-in-chief, Nicholas de Veteripont, might have been the occasion when boundary stones were reinstated around the perimeter of the manor.

The sites of five crosses are known on the boundary of Alston Moor; Long Cross, Blacklaw Cross, Killhope Cross and Shorts Cross on the parish boundary and, at the natural boundary, *"as heaven's water divides"*, Hartside Cross. Hartside Cross is now outside the parish of Alston Moor, but given the history and the topography of the area it must have formed part of the boundary at some time in the past, certainly in the thirteenth century.

The sites of the first four crosses lie along the eastern side of the Moor, with only Hartside Cross to the west, but there are no crosses on record to the south and north.

All of the crosses were placed in high locations on watersheds on clearly marked tracks, except possibly for Shorts Cross, which is in fact a group of three, one central cross flanked by two shafts, probably former crosses, all set into one large base stone. Pieces of the cross were found in 1908 by lead miners who told the vicar of Nenthead, who then had the pieces reassembled. It has been reported that another cross head lies somewhere nearby.

Shorts Cross is also known as 'The Bishop's Stones'. It is possible that the three crosses in this case mark the boundary between the lands of the Bishop of Durham, the Manor of Alston Moor, and Priorsdale. If the stones were originally set up to include Priorsdale, then a possible earliest date can be given to them from the reign of King John, who granted the land, through Ivo de Veteripont, to the Priors of Hexham in 1209.

There are also written records of another cross. On Middle Fell in the twelfth year of the reign of Edward III (1339) a wooden cross is referred to as part of the boundary to the property of Christopher Richardson. Then what might be the same site is referred to in 1713, when a boundary was ridden from the River South Tyne up Crossburn to Hunderbridge sike, then to the top of the fell where there was a wooden cross. From there the boundary went to Tullis Stone, then to a stone at Galligill Head, then to Greenheaps (Greengill Head), then to a standing stone in Nunnery Bottom and, "thence as water deals down Garrigill Burn to Tyneside". The route can still be traced on a map. This of course begs the question, were there any other wooden crosses?

It was at Hartside that a clue was found for the purpose of the crosses. In May 1929 the shaft of a cross of red sandstone was found, measuring 15 inches long and 10 inches by 11 inches in section. The cross had been wedged into the soil using shards of sandstone. When the shaft was raised from the mud, a small silver coin fell back into the hole. It was found to be a coin of Alexander III of Scotland, who reigned from 1249 to 1286. The bottom end of the shaft finished in a carved tenon joint, an indication that the cross had once been socketed into a stone base, perhaps a base that had shattered by the time of the possible re-erection in 1279.

In the early 1700's Killhope Cross and Short's Cross were moved "for the convenience of travellers", when it would appear their purpose was to serve as way-markers. But, as boundary stones to the Scottish Liberty of Tynedale, the crosses became obsolete as early as 1296.

The de Veteriponts in the 14th century

The de Veteripont family continued to be on the fringes of the law and at a trial in 1292 Robert's son, another Nicholas, was in Carlisle before 'justices itinerant' for some default but the penalty was deferred until the king's wish was known. However, after financial compensation from Nicholas, Edward I let Nicholas be, but the king still retained the mines.

Nicholas, like his predecessors, seemed to be out for his own interests. Another example comes from 1301 when he attempted unsuccessfully to deprive William de Veteripont, a minor and his second cousin, of his inheritance and estate near Garrigill. Whether there was any penalty for this failed endeavour is not recorded.

In 1296 John Baliol, King of Scotland, who was believed to be a puppet of his patron Edward I, invaded and devastated the north of England. Edward, known as the 'Hammer of the Scots', moved north to defeat Baliol and in doing so deprived him of all his English estates, which were put under the direct control of the English crown. Alston Moor, as part of Baliol's estate of Tynedale, at last became entirely a part of England.

During these troubled times, the ordinary men of Alston Moor were not only called upon to defend their homes, but were also legally obliged to bear arms away from home on the king's behalf. For example, in 1306 King Edward issued a summons to several men of importance on Alston Moor and neighbouring baronies to select 160 footmen and bring them to Carlisle on the Monday after 20th February.

Following Edward's death in 1307, his son Edward II (1307-1327), after various troubles, had to concede a truce with the Scots which did not prove to be permanent. On the 24th June 1314 the Battle of Bannockburn took place, when the English were heavily defeated by the Scots under Robert the Bruce and the north was ravaged by the Scots or else made to pay a heavy tribute. Nicholas de Veteripont seems to have taken advantage of the weak nature of King Edward II, for he defaulted again in some way, and was again caught out. At a trial on 10th October 1314 the custody of Alston Moor was delivered to John de Whelpdale, who would answer to King Edward.

Given the ambivalent position of Alston Moor, its proximity to

Scotland and the character of the de Veteriponts, had Nicholas's fault been to intrigue with the Scots? Yet, within the year he must have made good, for in 1315 the manor came once again into his possession. However he did not live ling to enjoy it for he died during the course of that year. The manor was then inherited by his son, Robert, who was a minor aged fourteen, and John de Whelpdale remained in charge until Robert came of age, which he did in 1315 when he carried out his fealty to the king. John de Whelpdale was then relieved of his duties and told to stop meddling.

At Nicholas's death it was recorded of his estate that:

"It was found by an inquest after the death of Nicholas de Veteriponte that he held a capital messuage in Aldreston with 14 acres of arable and 100 acres of meadow ground; 16 tenants who rendered 37s.6d. yearly; 33 tenants at Gerrardsgill, who held 33 sheildings and paid £5.18s. yearly rent; 13 tenants at Amoteshalth (Aimshaugh) who paid yearly £3.8s.4d.; 22 tenants at Nent and Corbriggate (Corbygates) who had 22 sheildings and paid £5.2s. rent; also one water corn mill, and one fulling mill, and 3,000 acres of pasture in Aldreston Moor".

Randleholme, the 'capital messuage' and residence of the de Veteriponts

The capital messuage referred to was Randleholme tower, the oldest building on Alston Moor, but which must have been relatively new at that time. Its walls are five feet six inches thick with an intramural staircase and a door in the old gable end for livestock when the inhabitants lived overhead. Nicholas held nothing else in Cumberland, which was a great reduction in wealth and power from the estate owned by his great-grandfather Ivo, who died in 1239. The will gives an indication as to the number of people living on Alston Moor, as the historian Wallace supposed that the number of tenants might represent a total of between 500 and 600 people. This was the same number as at the time of Ivo's death. The industrial activity in the area is noted by the presence of the corn mill and the mill for 'fulling' cloth.

Twelve years after the Battle of Bannockburn, hostilities between England and Scotland resumed. In 1326, Thomas de Featherstonehaugh was appointed "to array all the fencible men" of the Barony of Tynedale and the "Moor of Aldeston", to assess them, to lead them as necessary on the king's behalf and to punish any rebels. Then, in the following year, the new king, Edward III (1327-1377), had to bring a large army to the north to repel yet another Scottish incursion.

In spite of the warfare, royal administration of the area was not neglected. On 7th February 1334, Edward III confirmed the lordship of Alston Moor to Robert de Veteripont for a fee of 20s. and after this Alston Moor remained firmly in the family's possession until after 1371. Edward also confirmed the royal protection for the king's miners at 'Aldeston', granted at the miners' request because the original letters to the miners had been burned by the marauding Scots.

On 2nd November 1337 Robert was granted a licence to empark his wood of Wanwood provided that it did not encroach upon the King's Forest of Geltsdale. The name Park Fell has survived to the present day and encompasses farms named Nether Park, High Park, Middle Park, Low Park and a copse called Park Grove.

There is a possibility that the area around the present-day farm known as Mark Close, at the foot of Park Fell, near to Hall Hill, was the place on common land where the manor court used to meet before moving to Low Byer. The 'Mark' may also be related to an old custom of house marks by which, in the days before most people could read or write, a man's property could be identified to distinguish it from that of his neighbours. There is a gravestone in the vestry of St. John's Church in Garrigill of Cuthbert Watson who died in 1692 that illustrates some of these marks. Low Byer is a reversal of 'byer law', or local law, now known to us as bye-law.

Life in the 14th century must have been one of unending threat and danger from the Scots. For example, in 1334 the Prior of Hexham petitioned King Edward to be allowed the revenues of the church at Alston, using as his plea the need and poverty caused by the ravages of the Scots. He was refused. The revenues were later appropriated by Bishop Hatfield of Durham in 1378.

In 1348, while Edward was fighting in France, the north was so devastated by the Scots, led by King David II, that the people of Alston Moor were unable to pay the king's dues. But revenge was at hand, for later that year the Scottish king was defeated at Neville's Cross near Durham.

Although Robert de Veteripont was the King's Sheriff of Alston Moor, the justice he carried out seems more akin to Border Law than to the king's. In 1357 he, with others including his son William and John Parmyng the rector of Skelton, broke into the house of one Nicholas Skelton, assaulted him, cut off his left foot, and through grief caused the death of his wife and unborn baby. The reason for this act of violence and any legal repercussions are not known.

Edward III, while he was present in the north in 1356 to carry out another invasion of Scotland, reviewed the law in the area and commissioned an inquiry into the miners' privileges. Their rights had been infringed by the bailiff of neighbouring Tynedale, which belonged to Edward's wife, Queen Phillipa. The commission greatly increased the privileges, including the right to prospect for lead wherever the miners chose, and affirmed their right to elect their own executive official, but only in the main communities of miners. The king also wished to be informed as to whether Alston was in Cumberland or the Liberty of Tynedale. Even at this time there was still doubt at the highest level as to the position of Alston Moor.

The hamlet of Blagill

As a point of interest, it is probable that at least some of the miners at the time were Germans, specially imported for their skills. Germans are known to have played an important part in the development of the mediaeval lead mining industry. Blagill is probably a very early lead mining site connected with the German miners, who could have given it the name of 'blei', meaning lead. In 1389, Tilman, a German of Cologne, who had been in possession of some mines for a short time, possibly including the ancient mine at Blagill, had found them to be unprofitable, so he sold the lease to the Stapleton family, who continued to pay the annual rent of ten marks. Since the mines were not profitable at this time, the crown also lost interest. There is a further reference in 1478 recording the presence of Germans with mining interests in the area of Alston Moor who had to pay a duty of one-fifteenth to the crown.

Robert de Veteripont died in 1371 having outlived his eldest son Nicholas, who died in 1362, his second son William, and Nicholas's son Robert, who died in 1369. Nicholas had two daughters, Elizabeth and Joan, for heiresses but as the manor could be passed on only to male heirs and William had died without issue, the lordship went to John, Robert's third and youngest son.

In Robert's will, the Manor of Alston Moor was stated to be of no profit above its expenses. As well as the various tenements, there were forty dwelling houses called schelles (sheilings) worth 6s.8d. each and the water mill was worth 13s.4d. An interesting item in the will is the tenancy arrangement of one John Leker, who *"held a freehold of one messuage and one husbandry land by fealty and payment of one pound of pepper at Michaelmas"*.

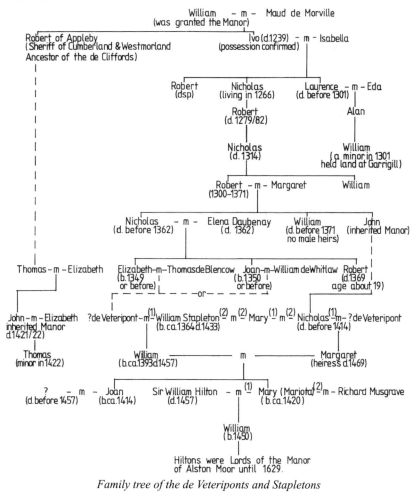

Family tree of the de Veteriponts and Stapletons

The Lordship of the Manor - the Stapletons

There occurs a forty-three year gap in the recorded history of Alston Moor, throughout which hostilities between the English and Scots continued intermittently. After the death of Robert in 1371 the next reference to the dealings of the lords of the manor occurs in 1414, when Henry V (1413-1422) granted 'the continuance' of the manor and the mine to William Stapleton at ten marks per year. This could be the same mine let in 1359 and which had been of no profit since then.

It would seem that the Manor of Alston Moor did not pass intact to John de Veteripont, but was divided up among the de Veteriponts on the death of Robert. As can be seen from the family tree, the inheritance of the de Veteripont estate through the female line, the relationship the de Veteriponts through marriage with the Stapletons and how the de Cliffords came to hold the estate from the de Veteriponts is very complicated and it is this period for which the records are missing.

For a few years after the death of yet another Nicholas de Veteripont in 1414, probably the son of John, the manor had been in the overlordship of John de Clifford, a distant and yet the only male relative, who died in war in 1421. Following de Clifford's death there were several years of legal wrangling in the Court of Chancery by William and Mary Stapleton, claiming that they should have the rights enjoyed by the Clifford family, rather than them being passed permanently to the de Cliffords, and in February 1426 the Stapletons succeeded.

The claim of William and Mary needs some explanation. William Stapleton had made two very astute marriages. His first wife, whose name is unknown, and who was the mother of his son, William the younger, was a direct descendant and heiress of the de Veteriponts, being the daughter of either Elizabeth or Joan, Robert's granddaughters, and his second wife was a de Veteripont and heiress for life by her first marriage to Nicholas de Veteripont, the last male of the line. William had also married his son off to the daughter and heiress of that same Nicholas de Veteripont. William Stapleton had brought together all the strands of inheritance of Alston Moor for the benefit of his own family.

When William the elder died only a few years later in 1433, he was still the leaseholder of the mine of Alston Moor, and after legal disputes between

William the younger and his stepmother, Mary, young William came into the whole property.

However, all this dynastic intrigue was in vain, for William the younger died in 1457 without a male heir, and after his wife Margaret's death in 1469, Alston Moor as one part of their estate, passed to their youngest daughter Mary. Mary was the widow of Sir William Hilton of Hilton Castle near Sunderland and the estate passed to their son, also William Hilton, who came of age two years later in 1471.

The Hiltons remained lords of the manor for 160 years, but left little trace of their influence. As well as the Manor of Alston Moor, the family had inherited the mineral lease which they administered themselves. The earliest individually named lead mine was 'Fletchers' near Garrigill, which was still working in the nineteenth century. However in 1475 it was spelt 'Fleccheroos' when Edward IV gave it to his brother, the Duke of Gloucester, later King Richard III, and others. This could have been "the mine of Aldeston More" owned by William Stapleton at his death in 1433.

Politics and Local Government

The Wars of the Roses occurred during the last days of the tenure of the Stapletons and an incidental effect upon Alston Moor was that in 1468 King Edward, probably in order to buy their loyalty after the wars, granted the overlordship of all his mines to Richard, Earl of Warwick, 'the kingmaker', and Henry, Earl of Northumberland. This gift included the silver mine of Alston Moor.

Relationships between England and Scotland were never easy. It was in the 1440's that Robert Whitfield, a native of Alston living in Sussex, was arrested on the charge of being a Scotsman. His northern accent, unfamiliar to southern ears may have had something to do with this. He was imprisoned and put in the stocks. Influential friends in the south had him released on bail but only until he could prove that he was an Englishman, so a plea for help was sent to Alston. Seven respected men there signed a testimony stating the Robert Whitfield had indeed been born and baptised on Alston Moor in England.

The Paine Roll and the Drift Roll

During the latter part of the 15th century, life for the ordinary people can be glimpsed from two local codes of law, the Paine Roll and the Drift Roll, that illustrate a strict but common sense approach to social affairs.

The Paine Roll was the code of civil law for Alston Moor, first made in the reign of Henry VII (1485-1509), and copied on several later occasions. This was a list of fifty penalties for breaching the bye-laws of the Manor Court held at Low Byer and was approved by the inhabitants. The laws were often those enacted by Parliament, to be enforced at local level; game laws, border laws, for defence and security, and agricultural matters. The list of fines was for offences such as breaches of the peace, encroachments upon the rights of the lord, failure to provide for the common defence of community, and offences connected with agriculture, such as the maintenance and regulation of livestock. A copy was made in Queen Elizabeth's reign (1558-1603) in 1597, *"with the likeinge and advice of Thomas Hilton Esquire Lord of The Mannor"*.

The Roll includes such items as, *"The Butts (for practising archery) of Aldston and Garrigill be yearely made before Sty. Hellen Day (18th August) upon paine of iijs.iiijd. (3s.4d.) for every default"*, and *"That noe man ffish without licence of the Lord or his officer between the Tyne Brigge and the foot of Low Crooke upon payne of vjs. viijd. (6s.8d.) upon every default"*, and *"That noe man shall marke any other man's marke but to marke and keep his own house marke upon payne of vjs.viijd. (6s.8d.) and not to make two house markes"*. Every tenant had his own private mark cut in stone, on his house or some part of his holding. Fines were commonly 3s.4d. and 6s.8d., fractions of £1, quite hefty sums for those days.

The document shows a degree of self-government in the north of England and it illustrates the troubled times in which people lived, since watches had to be kept day and night, with fines for failure to do so. As late as 1540, Henry VIII (1509-1547) passed an act compelling all males between the ages of sixteen and sixty to receive military training in the use of the longbow. Alston men would have practised on the area of flat land near to the town centre known as 'The Butts'.

The other list of regulations is the Drift Roll, which concerns the rights of way for tenants of named holdings for driving sheep and cattle across

Alston Moor to the fell. This was very important when land was unenclosed. By this roll, every man had to drive his livestock by a prescribed route to the fell pastures so as not to interfere with his neighbours.

For example: *"The Tenement at Lawbyare, Spinster Croft and the Loveings shall dryve over by the Cowstand band and through the Dubbard mea and soe to the fell"*. Sometimes even the days of the week were specified; *"The tenement at Blagill shall drive over Grugill foote and soe to the fell and alsoe over at the seamy Syke and over to the grene gill mea, and soe to the fell, and allsoe two dayes in the week and every Third Sunday up by the New feild syde to the poole and soe forth to the Grey Stones and soe to the fell"*.

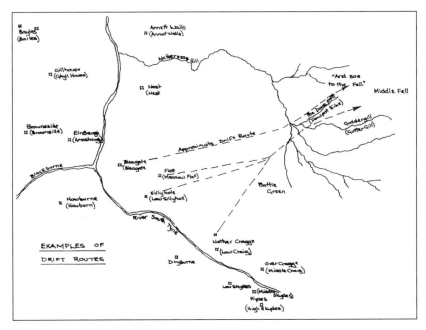

Example of drift routes

The year 1536 saw the start of the dissolution of the monasteries and in 1537, in spite of spirited resistance by the Prior of Hexham, the lands of the Hexham Priors, including Priorsdale, came under control of the crown. However, there was little effect in Priorsdale because the estate was separate from the Manor of Alston Moor, and it continued to be leased to the Lawson family, the lessees under the priors. Eventually the tenement of Tynehead became a separate manor with its own lead mines and smelting works. The dissolution also meant the end of the priory's interest in the churches at Alston and Garrigill.

Peace between England and Scotland was finally achieved in 1603 when James VI of Scotland became James I of England. Shortly after this, Henry Hilton, known as 'Henry the Melancholy', Lord of the Manor of Alston Moor, needed to raise money to provide his daughter with a marriage portion. In 1611 he began to lease off much of the Moor on 1,000 year leases, which is why several of the buildings in Alston have the date above the doors of 1611, 1617, etc. eventually at least 187 complete properties were leased out. These were often subdivided to eventually make a total of 260 tenancies which covered all of Alston Moor except Priorsdale.

In 1611 there were twenty-three tenements in the Aimshaugh district, while the number of tenements at 'Gerrard's Gill' was still thirty-three, and the number at Nent and Corbriggate was the same as previously, so there was little change from the population of 200 years before. A survey of lead mines was also carried out about this time and it reported that they were almost exhausted.

Henry Hilton mortgaged the manor in 1618 to Sir Francis Radcliffe, who had been involved in the Gunpowder Plot and was described as being "an obstinate, dangerous and not unlearned recusant". Then in 1629, Hilton sold the manor with all its mineral rights to Sir Francis' son Sir Edward Radcliffe for £2,500. The Hiltons however, retained a small interest in the area by keeping their advowson of the church at Kirkhaugh.

The Civil War

The Civil War touched Alston Moor at least twice. In 1642, the north of England, as well as other parts of the country where the old feudal order was strongest, was held by the king. His commander in the area was Sir Phillip Musgrave of Edenhall, near Penrith.

On an unspecified day in 1643, Sir Phillip received the following urgent message from one James Birkbeck, an officer under his command:-

"Sir, sonce I writ my letter heare came Thomas Walton of Alstonmore who reports for sertan that there is 60 horse at least of the pariments troupers in Alstonmore eversonce yesterday at alevon a clock, who hath taken Captain Whitfield & his lieutenant with many outhers of Sir henerie flechers troups before any of them were aware of there coming. Remeenes there yet ploundering houses and taking men presaners, for anything that is yet known to us // this considerd I thought it not amisse to send your best horses to Carlisle // It were everie neysearie that som horse and foot weare quartered beyond Eaden and som apointed for scouting in the night time especially for they com from where they ar into our daylles in 2 houres time // Intelligence is goon to Sir henerie flecher I hoop he will tak som cayer in this bussines for they sake I shall duble our sentre heare untill I have further orders from you //

James Birkbeck
They killed one man onely"

It would seem that Sir Phillip was away from home and that Birkbeck was acting in his stead, and Thomas Walton must have taken quite a risk of life and limb in delivering the message. One can imagine a lone rider evading the Roundheads and galloping at full tilt over Hartside.

On another occasion during the war, in December 1643 Sir Phillip sent a letter of polite admonishment to the same Sir Henry Fletcher for mustering some horsemen from 'Auston Moore' without authority, because Musgrave himself had that commission. Phillip Musgrave later went on to take Carlisle Castle in 1648 for a short while, before surrendering by treaty to Cromwell.

A by-product of the Civil War was the introduction of religious dissent to Alston Moor. With the Restoration and following the Act of Uniformity of 1662, there were occasional visits by Thomas Tailer, a Scotsman who had been ejected from his living in Edenhall near Penrith. Before him, during the Commonwealth, Nathaniel Burnand had held the living and vicarage of Brampton, then after the Restoration he was one of about 2,000 'usurpers' throughout the country who were ejected from their livings. He is rumoured to have moved to Garrigill, where he preached without a licence until 1672, when he duly obtained one before moving to Allendale. On 29th June in the same year John Davy also was granted a licence "to be a Congregational Teacher in Reginald Walton's house at Aulston More, Cumberland". Reginald Walton probably lived at Garrigill. Then, after the Toleration Act of 1689, a chapel was built for the 'Dissenters' at Loaning Head above Garrigill.

The Dissenters' chapel at Loaning Head, Garrigill

Agriculture

William Thompson, a local historian, in a lecture of 1925 painted a clear picture of peasant life on Alston Moor up to the seventeenth century.

"With regard to the communal life of the people, the following regulation in regard to the "Shields" may be of interest. It was decreed that every tenant that have used to go to the Shields do go the same within one month after St. Peter's Day (29th June) and there to stay until St. Helen's Day (18th August) upon the Paine of 12d."

"Sheales or shields were rough fold or shelters, adjoining an

equally rough cabin on the fells, where the inhabitants went to summer their stocks when the common fields were under the hay crop. In many places the lands that were mown for hay were undivided except for a ditch or at most a sod dyke, and except when closed for hay were stinted from about the end of August till the following May Day. So it was important that the whole of the stint holders should 'clear off' to the Sheales together on a fixed day. It would be understood that each man knew his own portion of the hay crop.

"This system of common fields and the division of them explained the importance of each man keeping up his portion of the 'head dyke', which would be the substantial fence next to the fells. The custom of going to the Sheales seems to have been a common one in those days. In Camden's Brittania (1600), he mentions that, 'here, every way round about in the wastes, as well as in Gilles land, you see as it were the ancient nomads, a martial sort of people that from April to August lie out scattering and summering with their cattle in little cottages which they call Sheals or Shealings.'"

In 1774 a writer in the Gentleman's Magazine who visited Alston and Cross Fell, in describing the scenery, said, "there was not a vestige of a house, except some old shiels, where in former ages the people had resorted, like the Asiatic Tartars, to graze their cattle – a custom now disused".

A dispute over the tithes in 1629 gives a good illustration of what type of produce, apart from lead, there was in sufficient value to be taxed this way. John Whitfield and his relative, Nicholas Whitfield, were responsible for collecting taxes in the form of tithes on Alston Moor when several farmers joined in petition against them. The cause of the dispute is not known, but, the testimonies were given as follows:-

John Robinson, on the 9th October 1629, in referring to a period of thirty years to his personal knowledge, and time out of mind of man before, stated that tithes for wool were paid in wool, by weight; for ten stone they paid one stone, and after that 15lb to the stone, after five stone had been paid, then half a stone, and if less or more, it was rated accordingly. John Lee, Laurence Lee and William Lee, all of Garrigill, and Robert Young of Ayle all gave testimony of corroboration, the last giving information about the tithing of calves. For five calves there was half a calf tithe, or the price of it as agreed, in this case, 8/-.

From 1662 to 1689 the government levied the Hearth Tax. Parish Constables were responsible for the compilation of lists of those liable to pay and gave them to the Justices of the Peace and the tax was collected at Michaelmas Day and Lady Day. People in receipt of Poor Relief or who owned houses worth less than 20/- per annum were exempt. The lists indicate the number of wealthy people in the area and the size and accommodation of each house.

The only account book to have survived in Cumberland is from 1664. Each page in the book is divided into two columns. Entries for a lot of districts cover several pages but the entry for Alston is contained in a single column. Unfortunately the page is torn off half way down so that only nine entries for Alston can be read clearly:

Alston moore in Leathward

(No. of Hearths)		*(Tax in shillings)*
Willm Richardson	*5*	*10*
Raph Whitfeild	*2*	*4*
John Whitfeild	*1*	*2*
Mary Teasdill	*1*	*2*
Nicho Whitfeild	*4*	*8*
John Laton	*2*	*4*
Chr Ridley	*1*	*2*
Tho Backhouse	*3*	*6*
Nicho Ridley	*3*	*6*
Nicho (Walton?)	*-*	

It would be interesting to find out where these houses were; the people were obviously of some consequence. However we can make a guess at a couple of the residences. William Richardson was probably one of the wealthy family of Richardsons who lived at Randleholme, while nearby Clargill is known to have been the home of Whitfields, originally from Whitfield in West Allendale.

Curiously, the City of Carlisle claimed the right to tolls in the Manor of Alston Moor, where cattle drovers on the unwalled, open fells were sometimes subjected to harassment. On the 4th October 1669, Henry Wallasse wrote from Alston to a Mr. Jackson, complaining that he had been "much threatened" by the bailiff of Alston Moor, and he asked Jackson to preserve his good name from being "damnified" for doing his job.

Aldston
October the 4th   69
Mr. Jackson
I have accordinge to my promisse sent you an account of what Droves of Cattle have passed thorough Aldstonmoore since last time I was with you which was at Branton ffaire notwithstandinge I have been much threatened by the Bayliffe of Aldstonemoore for numberinge of the Cattle and I hope you will not suffer me to be Damnifyed for Doinge the same
September the 1st   432 Cattle driven by George Casson
September the 2nd 286 Cattle belonginge to Alexander Lenix
and Matthew Ward
September the 15th 149 Cattle belonginge to Hector Graham
September the 25th 400 Sheep driven by George Casson
And this is the just account of all that passed through the ....
before Michaelmas and I received noe money at all (f)or ....
them and there passed another Drove belonginge to H(ec)tor Graham upon Saturday last being the 2nd of this Instant october whose number was 469 and if you have not the Custom this yeare ....
that drove I beleive will belong to those that succeede you noe more but my kind respects remembered to you and the rest of your ....
I remaine
your ever loveing freinde
Henry Wallasse

Animal rustling was also a constant concern. In 1691 the parishioners of Alston Moor petitioned the Justices of the Peace to act for their protection after the theft of eight valuable horses on the 14th May, even though the day and night watches ordered by the Paine Roll were still in force.

Social welfare

In 1683 maintenance of the law was reviewed by the Manor Court and the regulations of the Paine Roll still held, but because the document of 1597 was *"waxen and grown soe dimm that it was hard to be read"* it had to be copied again,

Consideration was even given to the well-being of the poor, in this the Manor Court laid down very hospitable regulations for their care. At a Court held on 22nd October 1683, it was decided that:

> *"1. We do order that the overseers of the poor of Alston Moor and Garrigill shall at every head Court to be held for the Manor of Alston give a list of all such poor as are within the parish to the head jury, that they may be present and order who shall go from house to house to be kept according to an order in this Court, and if the overseer shall neglect their duties to forfeit, everyone in whose default it is, 6s.8d.*

> *2. We do order and confirm an ancient paine within this Manor, that the inhabitants of Alston and Garrigill shall everyone, their night about, harbour and keep such poor people within the parish as are either so aged or infirm or so young that they cannot go about to seek their alms, and he that refuses to keep them, shall pay them 6d. to get their lodgings and maintenance with, otherwise to forfeit 6s.8d."*

There was also a system of payment for boarding out or maintaining children, for which the overseers were held responsible. For example, in 1662 four out of eight indicted overseers of the poor were fined 35s. for two years neglect of their duty in supervising the maintenance by an estranged husband for his child.

There was also a form of arbitration for unfair dismissal. In 1662 John Leyton was sued by Jane Vipond, spinster, for her year's wages, amounting to 20s. Leyton had turned her out of his services (without fault) before her year was ended. She was awarded 17s.6d. and costs.

At the other end of the social scale, an interesting example of raising revenue for the local lord comes from the nearby Manor of Featherstone. Here, every man upon his marriage, if he intended to set up house in his own right, had to pay a fine of 40s. to the lord, but if the groom was content to live in his father's house, the fine was reduced to 20s.

But the days of the all-powerful lord of the manor on Alston Moor were drawing to a close as the new century opened.

THE EIGHTEENTH CENTURY

The Jacobite Rebellions

On the 24th February 1716, Sir James Radcliffe, 3rd Earl of Derwentwater, was beheaded at the age of twenty-seven for his part in the Jacobite uprising of 1715. The Manor of Alston Moor, as part of his estate, was forfeited to the Crown. Many years later, his home at Dilston near Hexham was dismantled and the clock and bells were brought to Alston in 1767. The unusual, single-handed clock can be seen inside St. Augustine's Church, although it does have a new fibre-glass dial.

The Jacobite uprisings of 1715 and 1745 affected Alston Moor only a little. After the 1715, at the Quarter Sessions of Magistrates of Michaelmas 1716, it was ordered that every 'Papist' in Cumberland who had not taken legal oaths had to register his estate with the Clerk of the Peace, who made a return of them to London in the *"List of Papists or Reported Papists and Suspected Persons (1715-1722)"*. Of the eighty-nine Papists in Cumberland, there were Thomas Bateman and Richard Harrison of Nenthead, Henry Brown and Edward Errington of Alston, and Edward, Charles, Edmund and Thomas Errington of Corbygates. There was also Arthur Radcliffe of Capheaton, who was Sir James Radcliffe's uncle, who had estates in Alston and Garrigill. He registered as late as 15th April 1717.

Further to this, all persons *"suspected to be disaffected to his Majesties King George and the Government"* had to be apprehended. There was obviously more than one on Alston Moor, as the Quarter Sessions Order Book from Easter 1716 shows:-

"It is ordered by this Court that the Treasurer for this County doe pay unto Joseph Bowman and Thomas Dickinson, Constables, in Alstonmore in the said County, the Summe of Forty Shillings, for and towards their great expence and trouble they have been put to in Apprehending and carrying to Gaol (in Carlisle) *some persons suspected to be disaffected to the present government"*

There is no list of 'Papists' for the 1745, but there survives the *"Muster Roll of Lieutenant Colonel Fletcher's Company of Trainbands"* for Alston Moor. It includes *"William Walton (no arms); John Richardson (no arms);*

Nathaniel Yeats (no gun); Thomas Robinson (neither gun nor sword good). The last three are not sworn." In the list of Light Horse for the county, Mr. Thomas Whitfield of Alston Moor, together with the Greenwich Hospital, 'found', as in provided for, one horseman, John Vipond by name, in the proportion of one-fifth to four-fifths.

However the political upheaval in general had ended with the death of the Earl of Derwentwater.

The Arms of the London Lead Company

The lead industry

As the 18th century advanced, Alston Moor became increasingly dependent upon the fortunes of the lead industry, yet the inventory of the Moor taken after the demise of the Earl of Derwentwater showed only eleven working mines, with another four being "Nott Wrought".

The Manor was given by the Crown to the Greenwich Hospital in 1734 and it was under their stewardship, through improved administration, that the modern era of lead mining began. As the Lord of the Manor, the Greenwich Hospital proved to be an active and progressive landlord; it provided tree nurseries for screen planting and timber for use in the mines; it carried out systematic planting and draining experiments in the 19th century, and high altitude land was drained and greatly improved by spreading lime which sweetened the fell soil allowing grazing to increase.

The first main lessee of the mines was Colonel George Liddle who, despite his great investment and enterprise, failed to make a success of them and by 1745 his company had broken up and his leases were disposed of.

The London Lead Company, also called the Governor and Company, had had an interest in the Moor since before 1700, when it was first established as the Ryton Company, and gained a foothold when it acquired mines on Flinty Fell between Nenthead and Garrigill. The lease of Tynehead in Priorsdale was obtained in 1706 and further mines were acquired from the Greenwich Hospital in general letting of 1736. After 1745, when all of Colonel Liddle's leases were acquired, as well as the smelt mill Nenthead that had been built by the colonel, the company was the largest mining concern in the area.

The mines that 150 years earlier had been thought worked out, with a total production from the area of only 225 bings, or 90 tons (2½ bings = 1 ton), were producing more lead than ever before. The number of mines increased dramatically and from 121 mines in 1767, 24,500 bings (about 10,000 tons) were produced, worth £77,160. In 1777 when the Greenwich Hospital was leasing out 103 lead mines, over 1,000 people were employed, including women and children who worked on the surface.

It was during this period of prosperity that optimism in one case turned to over-optimism. John Smeaton, the engineer responsible for building the successful version of the Eddystone Lighthouse and many other major civil engineering projects, proposed an underground canal in order to discover more mineral veins and to drain those already being worked. Work on the 'Nent Force Level' was begun in 1776. When the Greenwich Hospital directors made a 'visitation' to Alston Moor in 1805, after £26,000 had already been spent, they believed it should be continued. Work went on for another sixty-six years before it was finally abandoned in 1842, having failed to discover the hoped-for riches. In the end it became known as 'Smeaton's Folly' and the final cost was £81,270.18s.11¾d., somewhat more than the anticipated £59,000. In the 1830's the level could be visited by arrangement with the landlord of The Anchor Inn, now the Low Byer Manor Hotel, as Thomas Sopwith described in 1833, "in boats 30 feet in length, which are propelled in four feet of water by means of sticks projecting from the sides of the level; and thus may be enjoyed the singular novelty of sailing a few miles underground".

Although the London Lead Company was the largest leaseholder, investor and employer, it was not the not the only large company on the Moor. Over the years after Colonel Liddle there were, for example, the Earl of Carlisle and Company, the Hudgill Burn Company, the Walton family, and the Rotherhope Fell Company that were also very large concerns.

The men of these companies were often referred to as 'adventurers' because there was inevitably a risk involved in their investment, that money might be lost as well as gained, and not all ventures met with success. Take for example the Earl of Carlisle and Company. For about twenty years, from 1778 to 1798, the Company, whose group of shareholders included the Earl of Bridgewater of canal fame, mined lead in the Tynebottom level at Garrigill. Initially employing an imported workforce from Derbyshire, the company was successful for some years, having found a rich, easily worked 'flat' of lead, but after that they did not prosper. On 26th June 1798 they sold out to the London Lead Company. It was this company, at what must have been vast expense, which channelled a new river bed for the South Tyne through Garrigill and attempted their own version of the Nent Force Level underground canal. The level was driven with a nine feet square cross section through the basalt for a distance of only about 420 feet before it was abandoned. The rock was so hard that progress was very slow and prohibitively expensive at £70 per six foot length.

By 1753 the London Lead Company employed so many miners around Nenthead that it began the construction of a model village, in which the workers could be housed and administered. Over the next 150 years Nenthead, one of the highest villages in the country at 1,500feet above sea level, was to have well-built, sanitary houses, a surgeon's house, a school, a reading room, a library, a market hall with a clock tower, shops, public baths and a public wash-house. The company promoted recreational enterprises such as the town band, a football team and, in time, a cricket team. The company also gave some miners land for allotments and smallholdings. This made sound business sense as they provided food against lean times and encouraged the miners to stay healthy and fit with fresh air and varied exercise compensating for the bad air and cramped conditions of the mines. All of which helped to ward off many of the epidemics suffered by neighbouring villages that were not so well cared for.

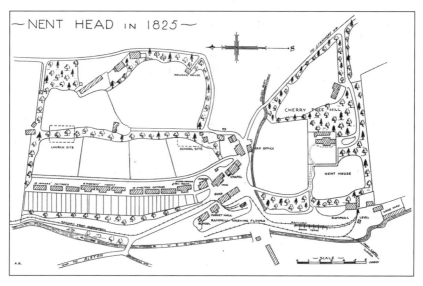

Nenthead model village in 1825

This relative care and comfort offered by a paternalistic employer meant that the miners as a whole were contented and the London lead Company suffered only three strikes throughout its history in the north Pennines.

The boundary of Alston Moor

To administer Alston Moor effectively, the Greenwich Hospital had to establish the extent of its domain. The lead ore fields, in particular the expanded Nenthead workings, crossed county boundaries and land in other ownership, so it was important to establish territorial rights. The Boundary of Alston Moor was walked by representatives of the Greenwich Hospital commissioners in 1761. The Receivers, or agents, wrote to the Secretary on 21st August that year;

"Sir,

In pursuance of the Board's commands of the 30th May last, we advertised for several weeks in both the Newcastle newspapers, the Commissioners of the Greenwich Hospital's intention to ride or perambulate the boundary of the Manor of Alston Moor on the 11th day of August, and the several succeeding days, till the whole was finished, and in consequence thereof, some time before we went into Alston Moor to find out and fix upon proper persons to attend and shew the boundary. In the doing of this we had great difficulty, it not having been perambulated in the memory of man living, though we were told before, when we wrote the Board about this affair that several persons might be had who attended at a general riding. We therefore went upon the enjoyment of the several persons on the respective wastes or commons which extend to the limits of the boundary, and found several old people, who knew that very well and by those we were directed in our perambulations from one bounder mark to another, as described in the roll now enclosed. Besides these persons, we had a considerable number of young men who attended us, that in case there should be any dispute hereafter, they may give evidence. These were persons who have no right of common, or are likely to have any without the Manor. From these difficulties, and the necessity upon these occasions of having a considerable number of people to entertain and pay for their trouble during the time of perambulating the Manor of at least seventy miles in circumference and afterwards attending to sign the bounder roll, the expense has been considerable, amounting in the whole to near Eighty Pounds, but as this was a necessary measure, and as the ascertaining of this boundary is a matter of great consequence to the Hospital, on account of the valuable lead mines within the Manor, which we are of the opinion will rather increase than diminish in value, we hope that the Board will approve what we have done, as all the care in our power has been taken to do it in the very best manner."

Altogether, eighty-one men took part in walking all or part of the boundary, and it is interesting to note that twenty-one of the witnesses could not write their names, but made their mark against it. The walk took place over three days, accompanied by banner carriers and musicians to announce and publicise their progress. The Boundary of Alston Moor as we know it today was confirmed, but not without dispute. In the words of the Commissioners, *"The freeholders of Priorsdale seem angry at being included in the boundary of Alston Moor."*

When the Commissioners entered the six liberties of the old Priorsdale, they met with opposition, firstly from Evan Emerson of the two Ashgill liberties, representing the freeholders, then from Jos. Hopper of the Tynehead and Hole liberty, and then from Mr. Hodgson of Tynehead and Hill Liberty. They all claimed that the Commissioners had no right to include their freeholds in the Manor of Alston Moor; that the lands together had been the Priorsdale given to the monks of Hexham by Ivo de Veteripont in the early 13th century, and since the Dissolution of the Monasteries had been accountable to the Crown, who had granted it to others and was now freehold and therefore independent. However, the Commissioners, acting on legal advice from the Hospital's solicitor, proceeded to include all the freeholds of Priorsdale within Alston Moor, their justification being that when Sir Francis Radcliffe assessed the boundary between 1618 and 1622 on his acquisition of Alston Moor, he had included Priorsdale and there had been no objection then. The response of the freeholders in 1761 is unrecorded, but Priorsdale is firmly a part of the Moor today.

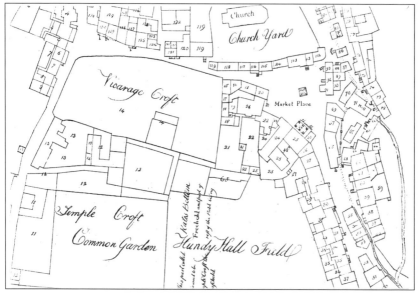

Alston in 1775

The growth of the town of Alston

As times became more settled and prosperity increased, buildings became
more substantial, and the 'Great Rebuilding in Stone', as Professor W.G.
Hoskins termed it, started, reaching the north of England in the late 17th
and early 18th centuries. Houses with datestones of around 1611 or 1621
relate to the date of the thousand-year lease of the site from Henry Hilton
rather than the actual date of construction. Buildings on the lower part of
Front Street have datestones from the late 17th century and house dates in
the Butts indicate building or re-building around the 1740's. Outside the
town there are many older buildings with early datestones, some of which
are bastle houses and bastle derivative houses. A bastle is a defensible
farmhouse with an entrance on the first floor. This fashion of living upstairs
prevailed in the town as well. Almost all of the mid-18th century houses of
the Butts and the Market Place had first floor entries and when the Back o'
the Burn was built in the early nineteenth this tradition continued.

Back o' the Burn, Alston. Note the stairs to first floor entries.

Buildings on the north side of the Market Square can be dated accurately to 1697 when permission was requested from the lord, Sir Francis Radcliffe by applicants with twenty-five other tenants acting as referees to acquire building plots for the construction of shops. Three sites were described individually, one of twelve yards by five yards and two of ten yards by five yards. When these shops with flats over were built St. Augustine's Church was obscured from view.

A map drawn of the town of Alston in 1775 by Fryer and Hilton showed that the Front Street reached uphill only as far as what is now the Fire Station, then the grammar school. Hundy Hall had not been not built, nor had most of Back o' the Burn. Instead, there was a mill dam behind the grammar school and there was a gap from there to Townhead, where there were houses on the site of St. Paul's Methodist Church and its church hall.

By 1775 Town Foot was much in its present form, with the Blue Bell Inn and Alston House in existence but the road bridge over the River Nent was upstream from its present location, approximately at the site of the old foundry bridge.

Townfoot, Alston in the 1920's.

It was not until the 1820's that Nenthead Road began to be developed, plot by plot, including in turn the Primitive Methodist Chapel built in 1825.

A lot of street names have changed over the years. Some of the have survived, such as Front Street, Kate's Lane, and Townfoot, but others have disappeared, such as Edmund's Lane, Thirlwall Lane, and Circus Lane. None of them received name plates, and even today it is only the post-Second World War streets that are formally named.

The entrance to St. Augustine's Churchyard, ca.1900.

There is a list of thirty-two shop rents for Alston that has survived from 1802 with rents varying between 3d. and 2s., the amounts of 6d., 1s. and 1s.6d. being most frequent. Interesting examples of property rented from the lord are, *"A Staircase"* rented by Jane Urwin and Thomas Urwin for 1 penny, *"Part of a House"* by John Hodgson's representatives for 6d., *"A Necessary"* (a toilet of some description) by Robert Teasdale for 6d, while Elizabeth Dalton had to pay 1s. for encroachment rent. She had obviously extended her property informally without permission. The thousand-year lease included a one pound 'fine' to be paid in two instalments every twenty-one years to the lord.

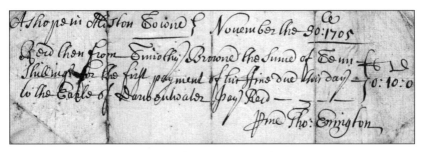

Receipt of twenty-one year 'fine'

The entrance to Hundy Hall, Front Street

Agriculture

Farming has been carried out on Alston Moor since prehistoric times but limited mainly to the raising of cattle and sheep. The altitude, climate and soil conditions are against crop growing. Corn mills of Alston Moor were supplied with grain imported from the lowlands, yet in 1729 a dispute arose over the payment of tithes when tithes of corn were taken in kind without authority by Joseph Ritson, alias Richardson, Joshua Mulcaster, alias Muncaster, and Thomas Yates.

In 1718 Henry Stephenson, Richard Wallas and Ralph Whitfield were the owners or reputed owners of one third each of the rectory and the tithes belonging to it. It was they who first demanded a tithe of corn and hay about six years before the dispute.

During the course of the resulting inquiry, information came to light about attempts to grow corn after experiments had been carried out in using burnt lime to improve the soil. It was attested by several men, John Kirton (age 77), Anthony Martindale (49), John Walton (80) and Jo Watson (77), that corn had been grown in a few places but in such small quantities as not be tithed and there had never been a tithe barn. They also stated that about 1670, before which time lime was used, several parts of the parish were fit to grow corn, including small plots at Crossgill, Dryburn, Fairhill, Low Byer and Wellhouse. There was also the evidence of ridge and furrow plough marks that corn had been grown anciently where it was not grown in the 1720's. It was remembered that about fifty years before a tithe of corn had been taken in kind at Blagill and Low Byer.

Then in about 1720 other farmers started to grow corn, barley and oats on a few acres at Bailes, Bridge End, Coatlith Hill, Hill House and Wanwoodside. At Hillhouse in 1724 tithes had been paid on 10 acres; for 1 cartload of wheat grown on 2 acres, 1 cartload of barley on 2 acres, 1 of peas on 1 acre, 1 of 'bans' on 1 acre, 3 of oats on 2 acres.

The time of this improvement was pinpointed to,

"... nine years ago or thereabouts (1718) or twelve years ago (1715), about which time one John Ritson converted part of a Cow pasture into tillage ground and wrought and gott limestones in Lord Derwentwaters liberty in the said parish and made and burnt the Same into lime and laid the Same within or upon the said ground which occasioned Some considerable improvement and from which the neighbours have made use of Lime within the said parish and since made severall improvements thereby ..."

In summary it was stated that,

"That the parish of Aldston lies in a very cold waste barren country insoe much that till within these last few years it was scarce known that any corn was grown there by reason it was generally soe wett and cold there that no corn would ripen in case it had been sown. But within these few years last the inhabitants growing more industrious and having found out the use of lime some small parcell of ground have been plowed and sown with corn (interalia). And by reason the tythe of corn was so inconsiderable in the parish that the plts (plaintiffs) lett all the owners of the lands in the said parish have the farming of all their tythes as well as corn."

So tithes were not paid on corn or hay but continued to be paid in kind on wool, lambs and calves. This however was commuted to a cash payment or 'modus' of eight pence or six pence or whatever sum as agreed.

Religion

By the 18th century the Church of England was becoming less relevant to the working people, including those of Alston Moor, and its system of hierarchy was beginning to be questioned. The most immediately noticeable aspect of this hierarchy was in the allocation of pews to local notables, for example in St. John's Church at Garrigill where metal plates at the ends of pews indicate the properties whose owners were entitled to sit there.

The religious dissent or non-conformity that had begun on Alston Moor after the Toleration Act of 1689 had blossomed. The chapel built in 1689 for the Dissenters, or Presbyterians, or Congregationalists, as they were variously known, at Loaning Head in Garrigill had been in use for many years until it became too small for its congregation and in 1756 a new one was built on the opposite side of the river at Redwing. This chapel still stands unused but in good condition.

The Dissenters' chapel at Loaning Head, Garrigill, as altered to a house

The Society of Friends, or Quakers as they are more commonly known, had already established two places of worship in the early 18th century. A meeting house was built at Wellgill near Nenthead in 1724, and that at Alston was built in 1732, although they were known to be worshipping in the town several years before 1720. The Alston Society was not isolated; there were many instances of the Friends sending representatives to East Allendale and Coanwood further down the South Tyne.

Although the Nenthead Society disbanded at some point, the Alston Quakers thrived and the meeting house was enlarged in 1764 at a cost of £13.12s.8d. The outline of the original building can still be seen on the gable wall facing Front Street.

Some extracts from the Minute Book of the Quaker Preparative Meetings at Alston make interesting reading. On the 18th October 1720 George Wilkinson gave account that his uncle Edward Taylor had left £3 for the meeting, 40/- to the use of the poor and 20/- towards building a meeting house. The monetary donations were known as "sufferings" and on 21st January 1742 it was requested that, *"Friends are desired to carry or send their sufferings to the monthly meeting."* On the 4th July 1770 the marriage took place between Joseph Bainbridge, merchant of Alston, and

Hannah White of Low Cragg. The marriage certificate was signed by the entire congregation of twenty-six witnesses.

However, people did change their faith now and again. From St. John's Church of England Records, Garrigill, on the 14th October 1731, *"Sarah, Mary, Isabel, James & Tamar, the children of Ralph Wallasse of Low Skides were all baptised the 14th day of October by Daniel Hudson, Curate at Alstone, being Quakers in their infancy till 12 years of age the eldest* (i.e. since c.a.1719)."

One of the most significant events for Alston Moor was the arrival of John Wesley in 1748. On the 28th July, he preached first at Nenthead, at 8 o'clock in the morning, then at the Market Cross in Alston at twelve noon, "to a quiet staring people, who seemed unconcerned one way or another". But despite this apparent indifference, Methodism soon caught on in the area and twelve years later, in 1760, the first chapel was built at Townfoot in Alston. This became too small by 1797 and the congregation moved to a new chapel in Back o' the Burn. At Garrigill in about 1763 they took over the old Dissenters chapel at Loaning Head from where they moved to their own chapel at Beldy in 1795. In 1774 the Wesleyans met between Nenthead and Nentsbury, probably at Foulard in a very small chapel on the hill, before moving into a new one on the site of the present Miners' Arms in 1816.

Of the earliest chapels, the old Alston chapel was demolished and houses were built on the site. The chapel, or perhaps a building on its site, at Foulard became known as 'Calumy House', where calamine or zinc was stored, whose ruins are rapidly crumbling. After a period of use as a mine office, the Loaning Head chapel at Garrigill was converted to a house that is still lived in today.

Perhaps this religious fervour on the Moor woke the Church of England out of its complacency, for a gallery was built into the church at Garrigill about 1752, and a new church was built at Alston in 1769/70, the predecessor to the present one, but Nenthead had still to wait many decades before it got its own church. In 1763, the Archdeacon of Northumberland visited Alston on a tour of inspection and he found St. Augustine's to be in a poor state of repair. Weeds were growing out of the walls, the roof was defective, pews were broken, and so on. He listed repairs to be made, but they were only stop-gap, because,

"As the present fabrick is so ruinous in every part that it can never be effectually repaired, t'is strongly recommended to the Parishioners to endeavour to raise money either by Brief or subscription in order that the church may be rebuilt".

A new church was commissioned by the Greenwich Hospital to be designed by the civil engineer John Smeaton and sufficient funds were raised for its construction. The main donors were the Greenwich Hospital, Sir William Stephenson, a native of Alston, then Lord Mayor of London, and the London Lead Company, an organisation originally run by Quakers and which maintained a philanthropic outlook. The old church was then demolished in 1769 to make way for the new one; the cost of which was £1,134.0s.10d. This might seem cheap but as the historian William Wallace observed, "It was not, however, uncommon to give free labour and cartage instead of donations of money". The church was about forty feet wide and, including the chancel of about nine feet, about seventy-eight feet long. The tower was about twelve feet square inside.

Law and administration

Churchwardens were the local government officers of the time and as bureaucratic executives their secular duties included such tasks as relief of the poor, overseeing the road surveyor and making payment of bounties for extermination of vermin, which included foxes, otters and 'fowmerts' (polecats). Examples of the latter duty are seen in Garrigill records, when in 1742, a total of £1.2s. was paid for foxes and 'foul marts', and on one occasion in 1747, 1/- was paid for two otters.

The task of overseeing the maintenance of roads was not always easy. All of the outgoing lead ore and incoming goods at this time had to travel by packhorse, or galloways, led by the bell horse, either over the moors or on unmetalled roads. These roads were the responsibility of residents to maintain and repair. In the 18th century, each adult male resident had to give six days labour each year toward the upkeep of the roads, or else be summoned before His Majesty's Justices of the Peace to answer for his default. In September 1769 thirty-three parishioners of Garrigill were summoned to answer why they had not performed their statutory labour.

The law on Alston Moor was upheld by annually elected constables, one in Alston responsible to the Manor Court and one in Garrigill responsible to the Churchwardens. However, the independence of the Garrigill constable ceased when the post became merged with that of Alston upon the formation of the Alston Moor Association for upholding the law in 1807.

In the 18th century, the Manor Court of Alston Moor was held at Low Byer, and every freeholder was liable for jury service. Freeholders included women, and less than a whole property could count as a freehold. Examples of qualification are *"(name of the freeholder) for a house"*, *"...for a shop"*, *"... for the other half"*, *"... for a part of (property name)"*, *"... for a ten(ement)"*. The summons for jury service were not to be ignored, as in this letter to *"William Uran at hogelridg"* (Howgill Rigg, near Gilderdale Burn),

> *William Uran I comand you That You Do not omet By Reason of aney Leaberty within my Baliwick But that You apear at the Court at Lowbyer on Wednesday 22nd Instant to Sarve in The Grand Jury given under my hand This 18 Day of october 1760 by me*
>
> *Thomas Walton*
>
> *(in another hand is written)*
> *rec'd the 24th of Octr   C R*

National government policy reached even this outpost of His Majesty's realm. On the 17th May 1775, after a special committee had sat since 31st March that year, the House of Commons ordered that a national survey be carried out of the administration of the "Poor, Vagrants, and Houses of Correction."

Until the resulting Act was finally passed in 1782 the Poor Houses had been a cheap source of very basic labour and were, *"prison with a milder name, which few inhabit without dread or shame"*. The practice was for the poor to be farmed out to employers and the Return to Parliament from Alston Moor in 1775 shows that it was not an exception.

In 1772 there were on average twenty-one inmates at the workhouse; in 1773 there was an average of eighteen; in 1774 there were thirteen, who, according to the returning officer John Hutchinson, *"were employed as the Master pleased and according as they were able, what they earned, we know not"*, and, *"The Master had no Salary he took them at so much a week per head in lieu of salary, and employed them for his own use, and maintained them, being paid regularly by the Overseer, once a month"*. The number of 'out pensioners' was increasing over those years, but by how many was not stated.

It was recorded of Alston in 1775 that, *"the house has been established between thirty and forty years, and there don't appear by any Book, ascertaining the Poor Rate at that time."* From the County Return, *"The House consists of 1 Kitchen, 1 Parlor, 1 Milkhouse and Coal Hole, 2 front Rooms above stairs, with 5 beds and Good Bedding, Garret Room, with 2 back Rooms and 3 ditto. One Cow House and Hay Loft. In the House is a Master and Mistress, who rent the said House with an Estate* (Fairhill) *of 24 acres belonging the Parish, who allow him 9d per head for victuals and fire per week, and find all other necessaries needful"*.

A later Return of July 1780, shows that there were nine inmates; an 80 year old man; four women, two aged 80, one aged 60 and one 30 who was *"with child"*; and four children, a boy aged 10 and three girls aged 10, 8, and 6 years old. The boy and two of the girls were brother and sisters and all four children were parentless.

Another way to deal with some of the poor was by eviction. Until 1795, parish officers had the power to remove people who were not native to the parish and were a financial burden to it. For instance, Isobel Madgen was removed from Alston to Knarsdale in 1731, and a few years later Margaret Walton was removed to West Allen township in 1739.

The eighteenth century had been one of economic expansion and political and social change on Alston Moor. Instead of a local lord and gentry at the head, there was a business which employed a great number of the available workers in the district and the London Lead Company was unusual in that it was concerned for the welfare of its employees.

THE NINETEENTH CENTURY

Census returns commenced in 1801 and trades directories became more descriptive from the 1820's onwards, which together revealed, in many cases for the first time, the lives of the mass of the people of Britain. The members of each household and their occupations, the professions, trades and services involved in making a community function, the schools, charities, and religious establishments, all these add flesh to the bones of statistics, to bring ordinary people to life whereas in previous centuries they were ignored as being of no consequence. From this point on, much of the history of Alston Moor can be gleaned from these two sets of information alone.

Occasional observations in the trades directories were made about the nature of the local people. One of the visitors described locals as, *"an industrious and loyal people, moral and intelligent, and of simple habits".* More detail comes from the 1847 Directory for Cumberland, which describes Alston folk as,

> *"...most of the men are miners, and by long continuance in the works they show a simplicity of manner rarely found among other labouring people; they are strong of limb, and when in liquor, a vice too frequent, they are quarrelsome and resolute; but when from home, are remarkably tractable, and steadfastly attached to their countrymen and fellow labourers".* They were of a kindly disposition and were courteous towards strangers; however, *"mining renders the people later in manhood, and unhealthy, so that the most robust person amongst that class seldom exceeds the age of 50 or 55 years".*

The Greenwich Hospital, the London Lead Company, etc.

After the demise of the Manor Courts the area was administered through the Justices of the Peace at the County Quarter Sessions, as well as through presence of the Greenwich Hospital. The London Lead Company, which was ever conscious of the well-being of the miners and their families, took responsibility for them through thick and thin, the result being that the miners were contented employees and there was no unrest on Alston Moor when there was strife elsewhere. For instance there was a bitter strike at

Allenheads in 1849, where the Blackett-Beaumonts were the owners, which led to a lot of dismissals, but this did not affect Nenthead or Alston Moor. In fact there were only three strikes in all the London Lead Company's existence in the North Pennines, the first in 1797, which was quelled when a company spokesman addressed the miners, the second in 1816/17, when Robert Stagg imposed his authority as superintendent, and the third in Teesdale, which did not affect Alston Moor. Another reason for this co-operation was that unionism did not exist. The system of 'bargains' between teams of miners and the company instead of wages meant that the miners were shareholders, after a fashion, profiting directly by their own efforts and at times of prosperity through high lead prices. The reverse of course was also true, and when times were less prosperous, hardship was great.

Garrigill village green (note the Royal Mail postman in his horse and trap)

The Company did all it could to alleviate the hard times; for example, during the food crises of the 1790's, and after the Napoleonic Wars, the company bought grain and sold it at cost or at a loss to ensure that the miners and their families were fed. It encouraged the miners to form Corn Associations, the fore-runners of the Co-operative movement, to which it gave money grants. In 1798 the company purchased the disused lead crushing mill at Tynebottom near Garrigill, to convert into a corn mill, which became known as Beldy Mill, so avoiding exorbitant rates charged by other millers. The miners established Friendly Societies to cater for the welfare of the sick, maimed, and widowed, but the retirement pensions offered were only a token gesture, as not many men lived to retirement age. This self-help was actively encouraged by the mine owners.

Miners of Alston Moor in the 1870's

The miners and their families were also given land to supplement their diet and their income. In 1834, it was recorded that the small-holdings rented to them by the London Lead Company were on average three acres of meadow and three or four acres of upland pasture. This was usually enough for two cows, or a cow and a galloway pony. The practice of renting land to the miners was copied by the independent Rodderup Fell Mining Company, on the Black Burn at the opposite end of the Moor from Nenthead.

Not all mine companies were so considerate as the London Lead Company. The Report by the Poor Law Commissioners of 1842 gave a picture of conditions endured by men at some of the other mines: William Eddy, one of the miners interviewed, stated:

"I went to work in Greenside (in the Lake District) *four years. Our lodging-rooms were such as not to be fit for a swine to live in. In one there was 16 bedsteads in the room upstairs and 50 occupied these beds at the same time. We could not always get in together, but we got in where we could. Often three at a time in a bed and one at the foot. I have several times had to get out of bed and sit up all night to make room for my little brothers, who were there as washers. There was not a single flag or board on the lower floor, and there* (were) *pools of water 12 inches deep. You might have taken a coal rake and raked off the dirt and potato peelings six inches deep. At one time we had not a single coal ... The breathing at night when all were in bed was dreadful. The workmen received more harm from the sleeping-places than from the work. There was one pane of glass which we could open, but it was close to a bedhead.*

In the winter time the icicles came through the roof and within 12 inches of the people sleeping in bed. During a thaw water dropped plentifully into the beds. In the upper beds the person sleeping next to the wall cannot raise his head nor change his shirt."

Systematic experimentation with tree planting by the Greenwich Hospital led to changes in the landscape; a tree nursery was established at Priorsdale and there were several plantations to cover the bare hillsides. However, the improvements in land drainage and fertilisation did not lead to a large enough increase in grazing to support the carriers' horses. Throughout the operation of the industry, the lead ore carriers lived away from the Moor.

In 1821 the Greenwich Hospital mines were yielding £100,000 a year, and lands worth about £1,200 were let, usually to miners. Although the London Lead Company was by far the largest, the most important and the best documented mining company, there were others. The Hudgill Burn, the Rodderup Fell companies and, later on, Jacob Walton were the largest after the London Lead Company. In 1824, thirty-eight companies leased mines from the Greenwich Hospital, many of which were very small concerns; twenty-nine had less than twenty workers, and twenty-one of those had fewer than ten.

A lead ore carrier with his horse, probably at Allenheads

The Hudgill Burn Company had a relatively short burst of great prosperity from about 1820 to 1840, with its maximum production between 1820 and 1825. A newspaper report of 1888 recalled that, *"when Hudgill Burn was at her best, more waste beer ran down the Nenthall sewer to the Nent, than is drunk in the whole parish now"*.

The London Lead Company purchased Priorsdale in 1820 for £7,300, and in that year it was allowed to lease *en bloc* from the Greenwich Hospital. This led to great changes, notably the rebuilding of Nenthead with the construction of Hillersden Terrace for thirty key workers and their families. The 1851 census showed that there was an average of five people inhabiting each house in Nenthead, with an extreme case of twelve in one house; a house normally being one up, one down and a lean-to for the scullery and pantry.

As the lead industry expanded, so did the population, and when the lead industry declined, the population followed. For example, the parish of Garrigill in 1824 had 1,540 people, more than the town of Alston has in 2010, and Nenthead in 1851 had over 2,000. At one time Nenthead was more populous than the town of Alston and had almost a greater population than the whole of Alston Moor today, but by 1891 the number of residents in Nenthead had fallen to a little over 1,400.

Agriculture

Although an important part of the economy in many parts of the country, agriculture on Alston Moor was very much the poor relation to the lead mines, but it was being modernised. In 1836 the Tithe Commutation Act changed the unpopular and anachronistic tithe to a form of rent based on the average price of produce over a seven year period, and the Acts of Enclosure enabled the further improvement of arable land by drainage, and improvements in livestock breeding were made possible by construction of field perimeter walls that are so much a part of the landscape today.

Enclosure had been going on nationally for some time. Over two thousand Acts of Parliament were passed between 1793 and 1815. The Act for Alston Moor was passed in 1803 and finally implemented in 1820. The traditional form of stinting, or allocation for grazing, of common land came to an end and livestock improved with the selective breeding that became possible. In 1820, private roads were set out over the commons. The Crookburn Moor (above the Hartside road out of Alston) Inclosure Notice was issued later, in 1842, followed by the construction of its access road, the 'Wardway', so called because the land was awarded to farmers and landowners. Wallace, writing as late as 1886, stated that Gilderdale Common had "recently been divided".

The combination of land enclosure and the coincident food crisis due to the Napoleonic Wars, led to a lot of high level, marginal land being brought into production. The farms of Leipsic and Moscow, just off the Hexham road near the county boundary, as their names imply, probably owe their origins to this period.

Sheep clipping at Howburn near Leadgate

The remaining unenclosed land was stinted with grazing rights allocated in proportion to the amount of enclosed land held, or sometimes a monetary settlement was made. Quarries on what was previously common land were left for communal use to provide stone for walling the enclosures. Likewise the common right to dig peat for fuel was maintained. This was sometimes used because the local 'crow' coal, a semi-anthracite, burned badly on open fires, and it had to be mixed with clay to make fuel lumps, called 'cats'.

In times of high prices, corn cultivation was attempted by the full-time farmers, but Alston Moor has never been an arable land due to the climate, the altitude, the lack of flat land and generally poor soil. Even in the valley bottoms, where the soil in the 1830's was described by Sopwith as a *"rich loam"*, there has only ever been very small percentage under cultivation, insufficient for the needs of the population. Fruit and vegetables for the

Saturday market had to be imported from Hexham in Northumberland, and after the construction of the turnpike roads consignments came from the Eden Valley and the Brampton area near Carlisle, although Hexham remained the main supplier.

To be Sold

BY AUCTION,

At Kirkhaugh, in the County of Northumberland,

On Friday the 15th Day of July, 1831,

ALL THE CROP OF

CORN, PEAS,
Potatoes, & Hay,

Standing and Growing upon the Farm at Kirkhaugh aforesaid, belonging to Mr John Maughan.

Consisting of about half an Acre of Wheat, three Acres of Barley, $3\frac{1}{2}$ Acres of Oats, $3\frac{1}{2}$ Acres of Peas, 3 Acres of Potatoes, and 23 Acres of Hay, the whole will be put up in Lots to suit Purchasers.

Four Months Credit will be given on approved Security, for all Lots above Five Pounds.

The Sale to begin at twelve o'Clock at Noon.

W. STAINTHORPE, AUCTIONEER.

E. Pruddah, Printer, Hexham.

Farm sale handbill, 1831

A hand bill of 1831 advertises farm produce to be auctioned at Kirkhaugh, consisting of ½ an acre of wheat, 3 acres of barley, 3½ acres of oats, 3½ acres of peas, 3 acres of potatoes, and 23 acres of hay. If these acreages are typical, then arable farming was carried out only at a subsistence level. The first edition of the Ordnance Survey Map for Alston Moor in 1859 was accompanied by a handbook describing the use of every piece of land. On Alston Moor, out of the total area of 36,967.534 acres, only 88 acres were put to arable use. The plots of land ranged from 0.114 acres to 8.669 acres; in only one place there occurred adjoining arable plots that accounted for 13.810 acres. Photo's from over a century later in the 1970's show fields of swedes growing at a farm near Garrigill for winter fodder. This rarity only happened because the farmer was a recent incomer.

In 1829, the little arable land that there was in the vicinity, was devastated when a thunderstorm occurred over Gilderdale, causing the level of the South Tyne to rise to its highest since 1815, when floods equalled those of 1771, when all but one of the bridges on the whole length of the River Tyne were demolished. Much soil from the valley bottom was washed away, and crops suffered very badly. Sopwith gave a graphic account:-

> *"On the 24th July, 1829, these parts were visited by a dreadful storm of thunder and rain, which continued the whole of the afternoon and evening. The sides of the neighbouring mountains, not withstanding their rapid declivity, were literally covered with sheets of water, which rolled down with resistless violence, in many places tearing up the surface, and in a great measure destroying the bridges over Gilderdale, Lort and Thornhope Burns. The latter was entirely taken away, and the former had only one wall left standing."*

The Alston Herald was a newspaper that existed as an independent publication from 1874 to 1881 and often gives insight into life on the Moor at the time. For instance in August 1874 it reported,

> *"With a great number of people there is a prejudice against the new mowing machine, it being argued that, as a rule, they don't do the work either so low or so level as it is done with the scythe, hence hand mowing is still in great request, and the few mowers who are in the neighbourhood are having a busy time of it, and are realising good wages".*

The paper reported a decline in the system of hirings for farm workers. On the 20th May 1876, *"There were very few present (Sat. last, 13th) more than on an ordinary market day, the whole system here having nearly died out."* And in May 1877 *"only two servants presented themselves"*. The wages offered were between £4 and £7.10s., or £8 *"for well known and tried servants"*. Those who were engaged for both indoor and outdoor work received from £8 to £9. Girls received wages *"in proportion with their capabilities"*. But, *"the town wore nothing more than the appearance of an ordinary market day"*.

Surprisingly, Alston Moor exported butter: On 28th April 1877: *"We are informed that the export of butter from Alston Moor is greatly decreasing. The reason for this is, that a very large part of it went into the County of Durham and not so much of it is now used in that County through the fall in wages of the miners who inhabit it. The price on Saturday last was 1/- per lb."* Then in October 1878: *"Wanted an agent in Alston to buy and pack about 1500 pounds of butter weekly for Newcastle and Manchester Markets. Apply to William Smith, green Market, Newcastle."*

Then the climate began to deteriorate: On 18th August 1877: *"The weather and crops. The almost continuing wet weather we have experienced for the last few weeks is making the farmers in this district very anxious about their hay crops. Most of the meadows are cut and the crops lying nearly all in a state of decomposition. Some few patches are still uncut. The crop on the whole is about average on good subsoils, but on others it looks thin and short in quantity. Potatoes and turnips are very little grown, except down towards Haltwhistle; corn likewise, but what few fields there are appear to be progressing favourably."* And three years later, on 29th May 1880, at the agricultural fair the cattle were below average quality due to the hard winter and having been turned out earlier to save fodder. The show of horses, however, was the best for a long time - *"small sturdy horses and ponies, suitable for the district"*. Rain was against the attendance on the day. Two or three card sharpers were seen in the town but the newspaper was not aware of anyone that had been "done".

Local milk producers were not above a bit of bad practice to keep their costs down and their profits up:

"Our milk vendors will have to mind their Ps and Qs, now, or they will be getting into hot water; indeed I am told two of them have got into it already. You mentioned a week or two ago that there had been hot competition between them, which had the good effect of

lowering the price, but it seems some of them have been endeavouring to make it up by potations from "the cow with the iron tail", viz the pump. Some half dozen samples have been got from as many vendors of milk in the town, and two of them will be summoned to answer the charge of adulterating this commodity with water".

Ann Goodfellow of Low Bailes and Ann Spottiswood of Skelgill were the culprits.

Agricultural implements at a May Fair, Alston, 1913

Fairs for livestock commenced in 1839 to encourage improved breeding. The fairs were held twice a year, in May and September, which were also opportunities for entertainment, such as races and wrestling matches. Later in the century there were extra livestock fairs, held in March and November. At Fair time, and no doubt at others, revelries would have taken place in Alston's 24 public houses. In 1881, this represented a ratio of one pub to fourteen of its 1370 inhabitants, with seven pubs around the Potato Market alone.

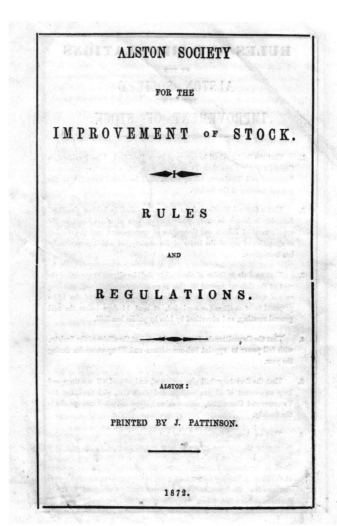

Alston Society for the Improvement of Stock, 1872

The last quarter of the 19th century was a bad time for Alston Moor farmers. The summers of the 1870's were wet and cold with little hay for the livestock, and these summers were followed by severe winters. In 1880 nationally there were heavy losses of stock due to foot rot, about five million sheep was the estimated figure. This was followed in the 1880's and 1890's by years of drought with more bitter winters.

Although there was an overall lack of land for cultivation, for at least fifty years, from the 1820's to the 1870's, the area known as the Holmes at Alston (the flat area where the sewage works are now) was a market garden of five acres or so. This was run at first by John Robinson, then by a family called Thompson, assisted over the years by the Featherstone family. The arrival of the railway in 1852 must have caused great inconvenience for the gardeners because the embankment approaching the station was built right across their land.

Poaching had always been a way of life on Alston Moor as elsewhere, and in spite of the severe Game Laws, it thrived. In particular, after the Napoleonic Wars, the economic depression hit hard and some men resorted to organised poaching just to survive. There is the story that in 1819 the army was called in by the Beaumont and Brandling Company to deal with an armed gang in the Garrigill area. The men were miners, and they 'went to ground' in the mines around Tyne Bottom and the officer in charge of the company of Hussars declined to follow them. The story goes that he was afraid he might get lost and end up in Hades. So instead he laid siege. However, the local women also knew the mines and went to other entrances to supply their menfolk with food, enabling them to sit it out. Eventually, the troopers gave up and called a truce. The poachers were let off on condition that they surrendered their arms, but all that the authorities got was a heap of scrap metal. The guns they received were worthless and the poachers kept their useful 'tools'.

Roads and bridges

In the 1820's, the network of roads on Alston Moor as we know it was established by the Greenwich Hospital via the Alston Moor Turnpike Trust and their civil engineer, John Loudon MacAdam, whose salary was £500 per year, a vast amount for those times.

Ashgill Force in a severe winter before the bridge was built

A survey was commissioned and it was carried out by the London Lead Company surveyors, Robert and Joseph Stagg, and by MacAdam. MacAdam was in his sixty-seventh year when he reported from Alston in 1823 to the Greenwich Hospital Commissioners, that he found the roads in the area in, *"a deplorable state"*, and, *"the worst that have yet come to my knowledge"*.

After an Act of Parliament in the same year, the construction of turnpike roads commenced. They were engineered by Macadam with the aid of a paid highways surveyor. All roads to Hexham, Penrith, Brampton, and Weardale were completed by 1829, and the road over Yad Moss, via Teesdale to Greta Bridge in County Durham, in that year was described as *"now forming"*.

Up to 1823, the London Lead Company had spent over £1,500 on repairs to minor roads and almost the same amount on new connecting roads. By 1827 a total of £30,000 had been spent by the Alston Turnpike Trust. When the Trust was inaugurated in 1824, it had responsibility for 130 miles of roads, which was an unprecedented size, especially compared with the like of the Brougham Bridge Trust, which had the job of caring for 1½ miles of road. The average of the 24 Trusts in Cumberland was 242/3 miles, and the national average was just over 19 miles.

Although by 1830 the roads were in good order, it seems that the bridges had been left alone and improvements followed later. Extracts from records of the Quarter Sessions from 1829 to 1839 for Cumberland, show that much work was done during that decade to bring the existing bridges into good repair, or else to build completely new ones.

The first bridge the records mention was on the boundary between Northumberland and Cumberland at Gilderdale Burn, when the County of Cumberland was prompted into action after it was indicted at the Assizes of 1829 for not rebuilding the bridge. The justices pleaded guilty, then immediately ordered that a temporary bridge be built and a new one started as soon as possible. Construction commenced in the spring of 1830, and was completed in autumn of 1831, the cost being borne by both counties. In the meantime, work had been carried out on Garrigill Burn bridge and Nenthall bridge had been rebuilt. Gossipgate bridge outside Alston was repaired by public subscription in 1834, indicating that what is now a quiet walk was a thoroughfare in those days.

At the Easter Sessions of 1833, the justices ordered that a new bridge be built over the Tyne at Alston, *"on the site of, or near the present bridge"*, the cost was not to exceed £1,400. The 'present bridge' referred to was one built in the 1770's, to replace the bridge washed away in the Great Flood of November 1771, when all bridges over the Tyne had been swept away except for the one at Corbridge. The Alston bridge was only some fourteen or so years old when it was washed away in 1771. It had been built at the present site, known as 'Holford' in the late 1750's, to replace a bridge that had presumably spanned the Tyne further downstream, in a location known as 'Low Grounds'.

Ashgill Bridge under construction, 1916

After sixty years the Alston bridge was inadequate for the needs of the 19th century, being described as *"ill-formed and narrow"*. Building work started in the summer of 1833, but floods in the winter of that year caused the bridge under construction to collapse. The old bridge had to be made safe temporarily, while stones of the new one were retrieved from the river and new tenders were sought for another attempt. Work was under way by spring 1835, and completion was made in the summer of 1836. That bridge of 1836, made for horses and carts, is still standing more than 160 years later.

The final entry in that particular record of Quarter Sessions is for 16th October 1838, when the justices ordered that £50 be paid to the Alston Turnpike Trustees for repairing the Nent bridge near what is now the scrapyard site in Alston.

The Hexham to Penrith turnpike road was the first to be constructed, and the first public coach arrived at Alston on 29th September 1828 on the new route from Newcastle to Penrith. Thomas Sopwith recorded, *"a band of music and a large concourse of people assembled to witness the first public conveyance that had ever traversed this part of the country. In the following spring the proprietors introduced a new and elegant four-horse coach from Newcastle to Penrith, by which visitors have a pleasant and easy access to the mining districts"*.

A coach named 'The Balloon' travelled from Alston to Hexham and back to Alston on Mondays, Wednesdays and Fridays, and to Penrith and back on Tuesdays, Thursdays and Saturdays, departing from the Low Byer Inn. The mail also travelled by this coach, replacing the previous service, whereby the mail had been carried by mules. This did not mean that the mail carrier's life was any easier. An item under the heading 'ALSTON POST', from the Carlisle Patriot of February 1855, reads as follows:-

"We understand that a reverend gentleman has applied to headquarters to remunerate the driver of the Alston mail for his perseverance in crossing the fells, overcoming the many difficulties in the shape of snow drifts, etc. The inhabitants of Alston will probably collect among themselves, and reward the postman for daily risking his life."

By 1847 the 'Victoria Mail' travelled to and from Haydon Bridge daily from the Blue Bell, and the 'Mail Car' went to and from Penrith daily. There were also several carriers for general merchandise. In 1829, their routes were to Carlisle via Kirkoswald, to Carlisle via Brampton, to Newcastle via Hexham, and to Penrith. There was a carrier service from Nenthead to Alston, once or twice every day except Sunday.

Alston Post Office

With the arrival of the railway in 1852, built by the Newcastle and Carlisle Railway Company, the horse drawn coaches disappeared, but the local carriers continued, possibly with extra business. Railways in general were serious competitors to many Turnpike Trusts, but in any case the vast majority of Trusts, including Alston, were in debt for most of their existence. As early as 1838, the Alston Trust had debts of £76,184, out of a total of £135,202 owed by the whole of Cumberland, even though direct competition from railways was never a threat. However, unlike many trusts, the Alston Trust gave priority to road repairs over interest and principal debt repayments. On appeal to the Secretary of State in 1852, the Trust paid no interest thereafter, and its arrears were abolished, which procedure was quite normal.

An Act of Parliament in 1862 empowered justices in the Quarter Sessions to combine parishes into highway districts, but Alston-with-Garrigill refused to do so, and instead formed its own district from a single parish. The Alston Turnpike Trust was dissolved in 1875, in keeping with the rest of the Trusts in Cumberland dissolved during the 1870's and early 1880's. But the roads continued to be maintained, and in 1879, the area was one of the few 'disturnpiked' road networks in Cumberland not to be refused a main road certificate by the Cumberland Road Surveyor.

Newshield Toll House near Alston

Of the Toll Houses on the turnpike roads, two are still in existence; one is at the junction on the B6294 of the Blagill road with North Loaning, and the other is at the junction on the A686 of the Hexham road with the Randalholme road. Those on the Nenthead road at Skelgill (at the junction of the road to Blagill); on the Penrith road at Hartside Gate (near the site of the ruins of Shaw House); on the Teesdale (at Nattrass Gill bridge); at the Clargill cross roads, and at Mark Close on the Brampton road, have long gone. They were auctioned off for their building materials in 1875.

Religion

Methodists

Religious innovation for the working class, having started with the Quakers and Dissenters, continued into the 19th century with rivalry between the two branches of Methodism, the Wesleyans and the Primitives.

The Primitives arrived with an eruption of new chapels. In 1823 they built chapels at Chapel Terrace in Alston (rebuilt in 1845), Gatefoot in Garrigill (rebuilt 1856), Whitehall in Nenthead (rebuilt 1853, renovated 1893). Nentsbury came a little later in 1830 with a chapel at Hayring, to be succeeded by a chapel across the river at Haggs in 1869. They also built a chapel at Blagill at an unknown date. In a slightly delayed reaction to this, in 1825 the Wesleyans enlarged the Alston chapel, built new chapels at Tynehead and Nentsbury and rebuilt the chapel at Nenthead in 1827. New chapels were built at Nest in 1844 and then across the River South Tyne at Low Brownside, Leadgate in 1848. Meetings were held in a house at Ashgill from at least 1848 and the chapel at Garrigill was rebuilt in 1859, to be followed by St. Paul's Chapel in Alston in 1868.

Townhead, Alston, with St. Paul's Methodist Church

The rush to build chapels sometimes resulted in shoddy workmanship. This is supposed to have been the reason why the Primitive chapel at Alston of 1823 was rebuilt in 1845.

Primitive Methodism caught on like wildfire on Alston Moor. In a book by John Burgess on Cumbrian Methodism, chapter six is entitled "The

Strange Case of Alston", where the author says that, *"Alston was the most famous Cumbrian Primitive circuit, the Moor a hotbed of Primitivism from 1823 when preachers via Weardale came to Garrigill, Nenthead and then Alston."*

At first the Primitives were identified with the general national unrest (this was only a few years after the 'Peterloo Massacre' of 1819), and that they possibly threatened social upheaval because, at their meetings, *"Their noise, merriment, groans, gesticulations and excesses aroused some concern ... but as their behaviour tempered their successes increased"*.

This was confirmed by a native of Nenthead, Chester Armstrong, who in his own book, 'A Pilgrimage from Nenthead', believed of the Primitives, *"It gave them release for pent-up psychic energies. It held out to the promise of escape from a 'vale of tears', reconciling them to a world of sternest realities"*.

It is interesting to note from the deeds of the Primitive chapel at Nentsbury Hayring that nine of the ten trustees in 1830 were lead miners, the tenth one being a blacksmith. These would indeed be the men who faced the "sternest realities" of daily life.

Congregationalists

The Congregationalists had evolved from English Presbyterianism, and they were also known as Independents. They did not benefit from the tidal wave of religious enthusiasm that there was for Methodism, but they expanded nevertheless. The chapel at Redwing continued to attract people from districts outside Alston Moor, but this must have been inconvenient for regular worshippers from Alston, who eventually formed their own congregation.

After a period of holding meetings in a room at one of the inns in the town, a room at the spinning factory was used, but as the congregation grew the room became too small and services were then held in the open air. Then in spring 1804 the foundation stones for a chapel were laid in Gossipgate on ground given by Mr. William Todd, the owner of the nearby woollen mill and the building was opened for divine worship on 13th February 1805. Once opened, Alston immediately became the dominant of the two chapels, over Redwing. The average congregation at Alston gradually grew to between four and five hundred, which led to the need to enlarge the chapel, the work for which was carried out in 1858.

As with the Primitives, religious ecstasy proved a great attraction, in particular during the ministry of the Revd. Francis Lamb, who commenced his duties in 1874.

> *"It was during his residence that a glorious revival broke out – a revival far reaching in its effects. On every side men and women were deeply convicted of sin; even while pursuing the ordinary avocations of life they would fall on their knees, and, in a paroxysm of remorse, call upon God for mercy, who alone could save them from their evil past." and, "Some of the greatest sinners in the town and district – poachers, gamblers, and drunkards – were converted."*

Mormons

Surprisingly, Alston Moor features prominently in the early history of the Mormon Church as one of the first of their churches in this country. This was mainly due to one man, Isaac Russell, who was born at Windy Haugh, or perhaps Windy Hall, near Alston in 1807 as the thirteenth and last child of William and Isabella Russell. In 1818 most of the Russell family emigrated to Canada and settled near Toronto. Isaac moved later to the USA and joined the Mormon Church after its foundation in 1830. In July 1837 he arrived in Liverpool with seven other Mormons on a mission to England to make converts and to encourage them to emigrate to the USA.

Because Isaac wanted to see his old home town and the relatives he had left behind, he travelled to Alston. During his stay of eight months, beginning in August 1837, Isaac was supposed to have been responsible for more than sixty converts. The conversion involved baptism by complete immersion in the South Tyne at 'The Dooker' at Bridge End Mill, Alston. In November Isaac was staying with his brother-in-law Jackson Wanlass of Alston Post Office and after his departure, twenty-three Mormons remained faithful, who were left in the care of Elder Jacob Peart, Isaac's cousin and a convert of the same 1837 mission. Jacob wrote to Isaac in April the following year that, *"The church at Alston stands fast in the faith and I trust is making advances"*. Jacob himself emigrated to the USA in

1841 and acquired six wives. Another convert, Peter Maughan of Low Crag near Garrigill, was ordained an Elder in Alston on 6th February 1841, with a certificate signed in Liverpool by Brigham Young. After the death of his wife, Ruth, in March, Peter emigrated to Utah in August 1841. Over the years he went on to marry three wives and to become a bishop in the Mormon Church.

The church in Alston was still going in 1846 when another convert, Ellen Wanlass, was baptised at the age of seventeen by immersion in the South Tyne – in November!

Anglicans

As in the previous century, rivalry from the non-conformists appears to have revitalised the Church of England. It woke up to the fact that Nenthead, which had a larger population than Alston, did not have a church of its own. So in 1845 Nenthead finally became a parish in its own right and St. John's Church was built on land given by the London lead Company. In Alston the not-so-old St. Augustine's Church, designed by John Smeaton and built in 1769, was demolished to make way for a much grander church, capable of accommodating 450 people.

In his design Smeaton showed himself to be a civil engineer rather than an architect. This is reflected in comments made over the years about the church. It was described in 1777 as being *"handsomely rebuilt"*, in 1794 as being of *"a plain but convenient form"*, in 1811 as *"a good church of modern structure"*, in 1829 as *"a good modern edifice"*, to Thomas Sopwith in 1833 it was *"a plain and neat edifice, the interior remarkably so"*. 1840 saw it as *"neat and well-built but without any architectural ornament"*. The 1847 trades directory saw St. Augustine's going downhill as *"a neat and well-built structure, but destitute of architectural ornament, erected about the year 1769, at the expense of the parishioners. It consists of a nave and one of those modern projections at the east end, intended to be as an apology for a chancel, with a tower"*. The chancel was after all simply a shallow, three-sided east end to the church. In 1858 it was *"a plain stone building, without any pretensions to architectural design or beauty"*. By the 1860's, when Victorian gothic grandeur was at its height, Smeaton's plain church was decidedly out of place. In 1869 it was rebuilt *"from the foundation"* to a design of G.D. Oliver of Carlisle, as a *"handsome edifice in the Early English style"*, at a cost of £4,245.15s.8d, but due to lack of funds it was without a spire. This was built years later in 1886 at cost of £1,000.

An anecdote is told in one of the trades directories that the church bell, the one from Dilston Hall, was cracked in 1844 by being struck with a hammer in a fit of over-enthusiasm at the wedding of two popular locals and the bell had to be re-cast the following year.

St. John's Church, Garrigill in the 1870's

In Garrigill, St. John's Church was in a sorry state by the 1880's. Rev. Percy Lee was vicar there from 1888 to 1895 and wrote of his impressions;

"When I first saw old Garrigill Church I questioned whether anywhere in the land there remained such a desolate looking House of God ... Of packing case shape; with comparatively low whitewashed ceiling; oppressed with an unsightly west gallery; the east wall was broken by a small sized sash window; three sash windows of a larger size broke the south wall; while the door and two windows, similar to the east window, looked out to the west; the expanse of the north wall was unbroken save by the fantastic designs drawn by the damp on the one time white plaster. ... The want of repair on this edifice can be gauged by the fact that I counted seventy rain stains on the ceiling my first wet Sunday."

However, Rev. Lee took matters in hand and soon work was under way to carry out renovations. On Friday 25th July 1890 the Lord Bishop of Newcastle officially reopened the much improved church. The church is known to have been in existence well before 1746, when it was old enough to need repair but Caesar Caine, Garrigill's historian writing in 1908, made an intriguing note that, *"Portions of a former church still remain underground on the south side of the present building."* So how old is the church whose foundations had been observed, and what is its history?

Education

In the early years of the 19th century there was a dearth of educational establishments on Alston Moor, but in this it was no different from most country districts. In 1805, only 209 children were receiving education here.

The London Lead Company founded its own school at Nenthead and magnanimously supported the establishment of others on the Moor with financial contributions. Once started, educational provision made good progress, and the Moor became well supplied with schools. By 1822 the number of children attending school had increased to about 1,000.

As well as schools at Alston and Nenthead, where schools still exist, there were schools at Tynehead, Garrigill where there were two, High Plains, Leadgate and Nenthall, one two private schools and for a short time in the 19th century there was a 'Ladies College' in Alston, which took boarders.

At Tynehead, pupils were taught in the Wesleyan Chapel, built in 1822, although William Wallace believed that a school had been held there since 1788. The school was built to hold 70 scholars and in 1860, the average attendance was 40. It was endowed with £25 per annum and received contributions from the Greenwich Hospital. The staff expanded from one master in the middle of the century to a master and assistant in the latter half. According to Caesar Caine, *"for many years (1851-1876) the Rev. George Monkhouse was the schoolmaster there, and very often do middle-aged residents refer with joy and gratitude to the days when they were his scholars."*

Boys of the 'High School', Alston, with their master Mr. William Cox

At Garrigill, the old Parochial school in the middle of the village was rebuilt in 1811, and it was later joined by a new Girls' British School built at Gatefoot in 1851.

Caesar Caine, who was vicar of Garrigill at the turn of the 20th century, believed the old school to have been in existence since the mid 15th century, and it was endowed later by the Fairhill Trust with £7.1s.4d. per year. There was also a bequest in 1685 from a Robert Wilkinson of £3 per year *"for teaching six poor children until they can read the bible"*. The school was another on the Moor that was endowed by the Greenwich Hospital, this time with £8 per year.

By 1861, the Parochial school was mixed sex and could hold 150 pupils. A Boys' School was attached to the Girls' School in 1872, when the school inspector reported that *"The Master labours under a great disadvantage from the smallness of the room"* where the forty-four children on the register had to be taught, and *"no time will be lost in erecting and occupying new school buildings"*. The local newspaper reported that the building was *"declared to be not only unhealthy but otherwise unsuitable for the purpose to which it has been for so many years devoted"*. In 1875, the schools were amalgamated to become the United Schools in the new school at Gatefoot, and the old Parochial School near the Church became a Library, Reading Room and Mechanics' Institute.

A small school at High Plains, about which very little is known, closed in 1874 with most of the pupils moving to the school at Leadgate. At Leadgate the date when the school was originally built is unknown, but it was rebuilt in 1850 by the Rodderup Fell Mining Company, a successful independent concern that followed the example of the London Lead Company. The school was also endowed by the Greenwich Hospital with £10 a year and it had sittings for 100 children, although by 1894, only 22 children were in attendance.

The school at Nenthead started in the 1770's in the London Lead Company's office, and in 1818 the company made it a condition of employment that boys between six and twelve years of age had to attend school, and that girls should attend between the ages of six and fourteen. These conditions preceded the government's Education Act by fifty-two years and even then the London Lead Company had a leaving age two years higher than that laid down by the government. Sunday school attendance was compulsory as well as religious attendance, but the choice of religion was left free. The company built was described as a 'large' school in Nenthead in 1820, with their workmen's children paying 1/- per quarter and others 10/- per annum. The Greenwich Hospital contributed £10 per year while the remainder was "liberally" made up by the founders, who supplied the books and slates. 180 pupils were on the roll in 1829, being taught by the monitorial system, but attendance had fallen drastically to a little over 100 pupils by 1847. A bigger school was built in 1864, which is now the village hall, described as, *"a commodious building ... fitted with the best furniture and most approved school apparatus"*, and, *"the best school in Alston Moor"*. This new school was itself was replaced in 1896 by the present school, built by the Cumberland County Council as an elementary 'Board' school.

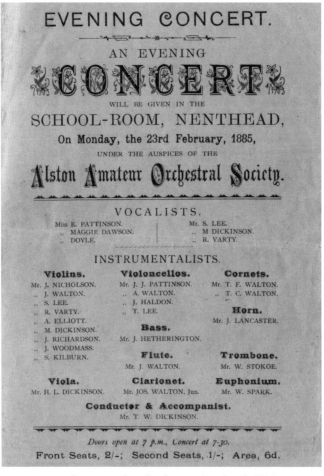

Concert in the school-room, Nenthead, 1885

From one ex-pupil's experience, however, his education was not ideal. Chester Armtrong in "A Pilgrimage from Nenthead" remembered,

"I commenced my school career (at the age of six in 1874). *I was taken the first morning by my brother Isaac, whose duty it was to ring the school bell. The school, I may add, was constructed much like a church, with an alcove jutting out from the centre, topped by the belfry in which was slung the great bell. My brother induced me to pull the bell rope, and as the bell swung I was lifted clean off my feet, much to my alarm."*

"School discipline was extremely severe at that time. Education appeared to be conceived as a hard preparation for the battle of life. It was a necessity, apparently, that it should be repellent. During my time three headmasters ruled successively. They were all alike in severity, ruling with an iron hand. One of them actually had an artificial cork hand, which came vigorously into use. On one occasion the oldest class of boys broke out into open revolt. It was, of course, suppressed, in the process of which the cork hand played a conspicuous part. The cane was the chief instrument of torture, and it appeared to be a special decree that every one should be treated equally. Being a tender plant, I suffered all the more. Very often I was unable to write owing to blackened and swollen hands."

"Such knowledge as we received was rammed home as if it were a disagreeable necessity. Instead of being made attractive, as it ought to have been, it was made to appear austere and hard. The internal arrangements of the school were of like character. The bare stone of the walls was unrelieved by anything that would reach the heart and imagination of the scholar. I look back on this experience as something I want to forget and cannot."

Bitter memories aside, John and Jacob Wilson, proprietors of the Hudgill Burn Mining Company, built a school at Nenthall for the children of their employees. This was a mixed school endowed by the mining company, who *"contributed generously"* towards its upkeep, with sittings for eighty-four children.

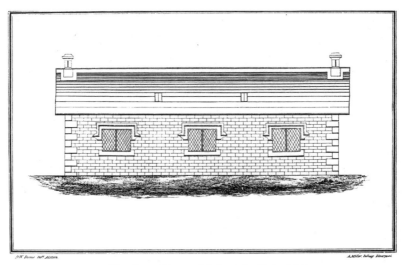

The Alston National School for Girls, 1844

At Alston, the old Grammar School, as shown on the map of 1775, was rebuilt by subscription in 1828. Its revenue came from the endowment of lands, amounting to the value of £34 per annum, £26 was given by the Fairhill Trust, and £10 from the Greenwich Hospital, which increased over the years to £45. Here there were, *"no free scholars, but the scale of charges is limited by the parishioners"*. Facilities were minimal or non-existent and in 1878 the school received a vote of censure from the governors because there were no sanitary appliances even though the school held up to eighty boys, which it did in 1847, but by 1894 the average attendance was thirty. For about forty years (!), the master was Mr. George Davies.

In 1861, as well as the Grammar School, the trades directory stated that in Alston, *"there are two or three other schools upon a liberal plan, for children and infants of the humbler class"*. The National Church of England School for Girls was built in 1844, to the design of a locally-based architect, Mr. D. Rome, and the adjacent Infants' School was built in 1851, also to Rome's design. The Girls' School was extended in that year by an extra class room, 15ft by 15ft at an estimated cost of £51. The schools, together with the schoolteacher's house, still stand in the old school yard in the Butts.

The Girls' School was funded by public subscription, and the greatest contributor was the local vicar, Rev. Hugh Salvin. It had seating for 150 pupils and on average the attendance was 100, which later fell to 48 in the 1890's. The town Handbook for 1889 describes the Girls' School as, *"a neat structure, built upon the most approved plan, and provides accommodation for 120 scholars"*.

In common with many of his fellow clergymen of the time who believed that one of the roads to salvation was education, and who sometimes took the entire burden of providing a school upon themselves, Rev. Salvin had borne the total cost of the Infants' School. The schools subsequently became known as the Salvin Schools. The Infants' School was described in the handbook of 1889 as, *"a large airy room, provided with a gallery and a classroom, having accommodation for 140 scholars"*. Attendance was about 100, falling to fifty-four by the end of the century.

The building beside the Police Station has had several incarnations as a school. At various times it was, the Free School (denominationally free), the National School, the Elementary School, and the High School ('High' because of its location at the top of the hill, rather than its educational status). It was described as a "commodious" building, built in 1811 for children of all religious denominations. About 120 boys and girls attended in the 1820's, each paying 6d per year, *"for defraying the cost of coals, etc."*. It was rebuilt in 1884 to hold 150 and by then the average attendance was ninety-eight.

Something of a curiosity is the Ladies College established at Low Byer Manor, and run by the Misses Walton, Frances, Elizabeth and Florence, the daughters of a lead mine agent, Isaac Walton of Brownside. The three unmarried sisters were each listed in the 1881 census as being a "Principal of Boarding School", and either business was not booming, or else the census was taken at a holiday, but there were only three scholars in attendance, aged thirteen, fourteen and fifteen, so there was one-to-one attention, and more, for there was also a governess present, twenty-one year old Sarah Caddick from Ebbw Vale. The college makes only one appearance in the census returns and one in the trades directory of that time. In 1901, there was another private school, this was at Park House in Alston, run by William Core, the former master at the National

School in Alston, and, like the Ladies College of the 1880's, it was short-lived.

A.F. Foster, Assistant Commissioner for the Newcastle Commission on Education, found in 1861 that, *"The lead miners are remarkably intelligent, and generally well educated"*, comparing favourably with the working classes anywhere else. It is supposed that William E. Forster, M.P., Vice-president on the Council for Education, took the London Lead Company's example when formulating his Education Act of 1870.

On 8th November 1879 the School Attendance Officer's Report for the district showed the following:

	No. on Register	Av. Weekly Attendance
Alston High	232	183
" National	62	49
" Infants	93	75
Nenthall	66	57
Nenthead	227	200
Tynehead	49	42
Garrigill	109	93
Leadgate	52	41

With regard to adult education, in 1821 the Greenwich Hospital recommended that a library should be established, and by 1842, there were four in the town of Alston alone. Each village on the Moor acquired its own Reading Room, and Alston had a Literary, Scientific, and Mechanical Institute, inaugurated on 10th March 1837, with a membership of forty in 1847, having 500 books and a museum of *"natural and artificial curiosities, and a cabinet of minerals"*.

Alston had had a library since 1821, housed in the Free School, where 500 volumes were available to the twenty-five subscribers and children could borrow books at no charge. Even Leadgate had its own subscription library of about 100 books, *"chiefly for the benefit of the neighbouring miners"*. Nenthall had its own Literary and Philosophical Society, established in 1845, with about 100 volumes. In Nenthead the London Lead Company, always concerned for the welfare of its employees, had provided a Reading Room, which is now the community village shop.

Charities and the workhouse

To support the needy in the mid-nineteenth century, Alston Moor had the benefit of six active charities, as well as the Greenwich Hospital and the London Lead Company.

Shield's Gift, dating from as early as 1617, was for the sum of 40/- (£2) per year to the poor of the parish of Alston, and was still going two hundred years later. Wilkinson's Charity, set up in 1685, was in part for payment to the schoolmaster of Garrigill for teaching six poor children to read the bible, part for the minister to preach a sermon at Garrigill on the 1st February, part for the poor of the village, and an amount for the four trustees of the fund. Stephenson's Charity, set up in 1757, was for poor widows of Alston, Garrigill, Kirkhaugh and Knarsdale, who received 5/- (25p), each on Christmas Day. Langhorne's Charity of 1802 was for the poor of the parish who lived in the Nent Valley above Nenthall. Charles Attwood ironmaster of Wolsingham, who had made his fortune partly from the minerals of Alston Moor and Weardale, in 1875 left £25 to be paid to the vicar of Alston, for the benefit of the poor as he saw fit, but without religious distinction.

On 9th July 1824 there was the first "Assessment for the relief of the Poor and for other purposes in the Acts of Parliament mentioned relating to the Poor of the Parish of Alston in the County of Cumberland". The rate was one shilling in the pound, or five pence in the pound as it would be today, which raised £355.16s.10d.

The Fairhill Estates Charity was a much more elaborate charity, and it led to the establishment of the Workhouse. It exists today as a grant-giving body whose present trustees are the Parish Council. Caesar Caine described how in 1739, several sums of money had been bequeathed to the poor, and to schools in the parish of Alston with Garrigill. In order to secure these funds, a tenement and its appurtenances was purchased at Nether Fairhill, as well as a fourth part of a pasture called Fairhill. The whole was let and the rental money of £274 was available for distribution. The estate was let to the highest bidder, who 'farmed' the poor, by hiring out their labour, and taking care of them in the workhouse situated on the estate. In 1818, the estate was let for £30 per year, and the poor were maintained at 2s.10d. each per week. In 1819, the rent was £35, and the poor cost 2s.8d. per week, and later the rent was £36.10s., and the poor were maintained at 2s.5d. per week. More money was coming in, but less money was spent on the poor.

The Workhouse was built to accommodate eighty people, but the greatest number of inmates recorded at any census was thirty-eight, and the least was twenty. It was run by a Master and Matron, usually husband and wife, but at one time a mother and son were in charge, after the husband had died. On another occasion a man and woman in no registered relationship were Master and Matron. There was also an Assistant Overseer, a Relieving Officer, a Medical Officer, and an Honorary Chaplain.

One of the aims of the New Poor Law of 1834 was that the poor should be as little of a burden as possible on the parish - all relief was to be issued through the Workhouse and the inmates had to make a profit if at all possible. In 1858, the income was £1502.18s., with an expenditure of £1648. In 1847 the cost of maintaining an inmate had decreased still further to 2s. per week, but in 1884, the lavish sum of 3s.4d. was spent per head per week.

An example of the administration of the Workhouse later in the century, comes from the minutes of the fortnightly meeting of the Board of Guardians held at the Town Hall in November 1875, when:-

"The clerk handed in a bill for £7.5s., from the Royal Albert Asylum, Lancaster, for the maintenance of one inmate belonging to this parish for the quarter ending December next. It was ordered to be paid, as was also a charge of 14s. to the Relieving Officer for expenses in conveying a lunatic to Garlands Asylum (in Carlisle). *The clerk reported that a lunacy inspector had visited the Workhouse, but had not made any remarks, and Mrs. Walton had also visited the house during the week.*

The Master of the Workhouse reported that Smith Elliot had been striking one of the other inmates and also himself and he had had to be put in a refractory ward (a cell by any other name). *Mr. Hutchinson referred to a case of a young woman, who, he thought, might be able to take a situation if she was a little more advanced in education. She was lame of her left hand, but her right hand was good. It was agreed that she be requested to attend school."*

Industries

The town of Alston was the service centre for the whole of Alston Moor. Through the trades directories of Cumberland for about a hundred years between 1829 and 1938 the various industries, trades and crafts come to light. As well as the boot, shoe and patten (wooden sole) makers, milliners, drapers, grocers, tea merchants, blacksmiths, butchers, tailors, and other one-man businesses to be found in any town of that time, there are more unusual skills, and manufacturers who employed a workforce.

Lead shot manufacturing

Early in the 19th century, with only a brief entry in the directory of 1829, there was a lead shot tower at Tower Hill in Alston, on the opposite side of the River Tyne to the Tyne Willows. Thomas Sopwith described it as being, *"with embrasures at the top, and a house adjoining, has much the appearance of a church. It is 56 feet high, and is built over a shaft of nearly the same depth.* The shot is brought out by a level at the base of the steep hill on which the tower is built". The factory was owned by John Dryden who was listed in 1829 as an ironmonger and patent shot manufacturer, but by 1834 he was an ironmonger only, so it would seem that the factory closed between 1829 and 1834. The building was converted into a house and all traces of the tower are gone.

Clockmakers

About fourteen clocks are known to have survived that were made by Alston clockmakers, of which there were approximately twenty between the eighteenth and nineteenth centuries. The period when they were most numerous seems to have been the 1840's, when six clockmakers were in business.

One or two clockmakers are described as having great ingenuity. For example Joseph Hall, who lived and worked in Alston around the turn of the 19th century, made a clock that played twelve tunes and showed the phases of the moon, as well as another clock that showed the month, the date, phases of the moon, sunrise, sunset, and Saints Days. There was also James Kirton who was amongst the earliest clockmakers in Cumberland.

He died on 30th May 1729 aged 43. The Burials Register reads, *"James Kirton, the ingenious clockmaker of Alston, buried 1st June 1729."*

Five of Hall's clocks are known and of the other clockmakers, three clocks are known to have been made by John Craig of Ashgillside, six other makers have one clock each, and a further nine makers, including Hugh Lee Pattinson, discoverer of the lead de-silvering process, have no surviving clocks. It seems likely that their business was in repairing rather than manufacturing.

Corn millers

Alston Moor possessed five corn mills, two of which were still working in the 20th century, two disappeared from the records in the 1860's, and the other one in the 1880's. Four of the mill buildings still exist, and as purpose-made manufactories, apart from Beldy, they occupy a special place in the history of the Moor.

Beldy Mill in Garrigill was an old lead crushing mill bought in 1798 by the London Lead Company and converted into a corn mill for the benefit of the miners. For a few years prior to this, the Company had imported rye and corn grain to the area and sold it to the miners and their families at cost price. This was because of the food crisis caused by the wars with France at that time. In particular there was a shortage of bread which was aggravated by the exorbitant prices charged by local millers for grinding the grain into bread flour. Once the new mill was in operation, grain was ground better than at its rivals and it was also cheaper. However the distress was not only with the miners, but with all of the community on Alston Moor, so the mill was soon opened to everyone, which brought down charges at the other mills. Later, Beldy Mill was handed over to the management of a Corn Association of the Company's workmen. From 1829 there was a succession of millers, none staying for much longer than ten years or so, until 1884, after which year it ceased to be listed in the Trade Directories.

The oldest documented corn mill is Blackburn Mill at Leadgate which is known to have been in existence in 1590 when it was owned by Thomas Vipond. Church registers give the names of many of the occupants during the eighteenth century and in 1802 it was let to William Todd. It appears in the 1829 trades directory with John Bell as the miller. In 1834 George Thompson was the miller of 'Bell's Mill'. Leadgate may seem a quiet, out-of-the way spot today, but before McAdam's turnpike road was made in the 1820's, most traffic to and from Alston, Garrigill, Nenthead, and Tynehead, which were far more populous settlements than now, had to pass through Leadgate in order to reach Penrith and the Eden Valley. Some travellers and merchandise, however, went via Cross Fell, and as late as 1881, repairs to that road were ordered by the Rural Sanitary Board. The name of Leadgate means 'lead road', and the hamlet would have been a bustling thoroughfare, as well as being home to the miners and their families of the nearby Rotherhope, or Rodderup Mine. For ten years or more from about 1841 to 1851, Joseph Pearson was the miller, and he employed one other worker in the mill, who 'lived in'. Pearson was followed by W. Thompson, miller in 1861, but after this it disappears from the records as a working mill.

Bridge End corn mill

Bridge End Mill near Alston was a family business during the 19th century. It was operated for about thirty years by Timothy Welsh, who also farmed Bridge End Farm, and later he worked it in partnership with his son, William. Then, like Blackburn Mill, there is no further mention of it after 1861. Perhaps both mills succumbed to cheaper, mass produced flour brought in by the railway. The mill race, the site of the sluice gates, and posts in the river on the site of the weir, can still be seen at Bridge End Mill. The building itself still exists, but it is a ruin in danger of collapse.

Low Mill in Alston was built sometime before 1766, when Robert Hodgson was the owner. It remained in operation until the 1950's, when it was known as Haldon's Mill. In 1814 Joseph Hall bought the mill from Robert Hodgson's son, Robert, for £740. He sold it in 1825 for £1050 to Esther Vipond, a widow whose son Utrick (a Christian name not uncommon on Alston Moor of old), was the miller who employed three men in the 1850's. In the 1860's the mill was bought by Matthew Whitfield, followed by his son Samuel, who was miller until the first years of the 20th century. As well as being millers, most of the millers of the Low Mill doubled as grocers and corn merchants. The overshot wheel was 29 feet 6 inches in diameter and 10 inches wide and produced about ten horsepower. On the town map of 1775, when Robert Hodgson was the proprietor, the long axis of the mill building is shown at right angles to the mill race, which at that point is on a subsidiary of the main mill stream that ran through the town. The site on Station Road is an open grassed area.

The best known and best documented corn mill is the High Mill, near the Market Place in Alston, the wheel-house of which is still intact, complete with the wheel. It could be the site of the mill listed in the will of Nicholas de Veteripont in 1315. Certainly its location is the most convenient for the townspeople, and for obtaining a head of water for power. Nevertheless, there were occasions when, in spite of the mill dam which can still be seen up on the Fairhill, water was in short supply.

The High Mill was listed in the inventory of James, Earl of Derwentwater, as rented to Richard Wallace, for the sum of £60.7s.6d. per year. In 1767 it was completely rebuilt by John Smeaton, the engineer famous for building the successful version of the Eddystone Lighthouse, the Nent Force Level, and who was involved in sinking shafts at Rotherhope Mine. In 1775, it was let by the Greenwich Hospital to Adam Wilkinson at a rent of £30 per annum, and in 1800 it was let to William

Todd at £42 p.a., then in 1817 to William Greenwell and Co. From the 1820's to the 1840's Hetherington and Peart owned it, and in the 1850's and 1860's, Robert Nattrass was the miller, employing four men, followed by John Lancaster, who had been an employee of Robert Nattrass. John Lancaster died in 1872 at the early age of 45, and was succeeded by his son Joseph, who was also a bacon curer. Joseph was followed in turn, after his death at the age of 60 in December 1909, by his son, John. Because of this family succession, the High Mill was often referred to as 'Lancaster's Mill'.

Haldon's shop on Station Road, opposite where the Low Mill stood

Snippets of information about the state of the mill survive from 1858 and 1859. In December 1858 the mill was offered for the rent of £65, *"without the steam engine apparatus"*, and the next year two millwrights from Hexham reported that the building was in need of repair and alteration. The mill dam on the Fairhill was cleaned out, new supply pipes were laid under the street and a watercourse from Nattrass Gill to the mill dam was installed, the *"steam engine, etc."* was removed to be replaced by oatmeal kilns, and walls and the roof were repaired. This was all finished by

December. A remnant of the outdoor overhead water supply can be seen by a stone bracket that supported the wooden leat in the wall over the wheelhouse

In general, corn milling changed in the 1870's with the introduction of roller milling for which harder, imported grains were more suitable than the soft English wheat, and the remaining Alston mills concentrated more on producing animal feed.

The brewery

Even though it ceased to be a brewery in the 1880's, the complex of buildings beside the Tyne Bridge is still referred to as 'The Brewery'. The earliest reference to a brewery in Alston is in the 'Brew Rent' of 15 shillings owed to the Earl of Derwentwater in 1699. In 1782 land was transferred to Christopher Blackett and Partners, as well as the George and Dragon in the Potato Market, Alston, and Cherry Tree House in Nenthead. Westgarth Forster of Allenheads, the father of the Westgarth Forster of 'Treatise' fame, was one of the original partners. The brewery was built in the same year with water obtained from a spring at Black House Well not far away. It was well established in the 1820's as Christopher Blackett & Co. In 1834 John Gill was a *"retailer of beer"* and by 1847 the brewery was owned by Shaw, Gill, & Co, when three brewers and a labourer were employed, but soon John Gill was the sole proprietor. In 1853 it was one of 2,470 registered breweries in the country.

A sad story is connected with the Brewery. On the 6th May 1852, Mary, an orphan whose surname was unknown, who lived with the brewer William Craig and his family, threw herself off the nearby South Tyne Bridge.

South Tyne Bridge and the Brewery
Note on the right that the tower and the building with the chimney have been demolished.

In 1869, Railton Gill & Co. Brewers and Maltsters appeared in the Trade Directory. Railton Gill was John Gill's younger brother and also a surgeon who had qualified in Edinburgh. He probably acquired the brewery on John's death in 1852 at the early age of 43 and ran the brewery through his agent William Maughan and the chief brewer, Thomas Hall, who was succeeded by Thomas Brown. From the 1870's until its closure in the 1880's another John Gill, son of the first John Gill, was the owner who employed four labourers. The younger John Gill was in partnership with his brother George, and when the firm ceased operations the cause was supposed to have been because the brothers drank themselves out of business. George at least seems to have been a sad figure. For a few years in the 1870's, perhaps when times were full of optimism, he lived in the grand Georgian-style house of Harbut Lodge on the Brampton road, but he soon left, as things started to go wrong. His wife died in 1881 when she was 28 years old, then the brewery failed, and in the 1891 census he is described as a retired brewer boarding at the Blue Bell Inn. He died the following year at the age of 44.

Independent Order of Rechabites, 1913

Opposed to the brewery was the teetotal Independent Order of Rechabites, a society with many members who had a meeting house at Overwater in Nenthead and organised society events such as charabanc outings as an alternative to the evils of drink.

After the demise of the brewery, the building became a stocking factory under the management of George William Storey, whose employees made woollen stockings for the miners. An elderly resident remembered that *"the women used to come out with armfuls of stockings (in tube form) and take them home and they got so much for each stocking for sewing the toes and heels up"*.

Tile making

There have been at least two attempts to establish a field drainage tile factory on Alston Moor. Production of this commodity seems logical given that the subsoil is boulder clay, but neither attempt lasted very long. From 1853 to 1855 there was a tilery near Skelgill on the Nenthead road from Alston, and then another one commenced in June 1866 at How Hill on the road junction to Garrigill with the Middleton road. At first the later one met with success. Part of a letter of October 18th 1866 from J.M. Paull, the Moormaster for the Greenwich Hospital, reads, *"I beg to inform you that having exposed some tiles from How hill tilery to the action of water for a month and found they have in no way been softened by the exposure I think we might venture on commencing to drain with them on Shawside farm and I think of making a beginning early next week"*. Even so, drainage tiles still had to be brought into Alston Moor via the railway station.

And then the enterprise appears not to have been successful, for a letter from J.M. Paull, the Moormaster on February 1st 1868 reads *"I suppose we must get those drain pipes that will be required for Randalholme from Featherstone as there are no more at the How Hill works"*. His words "no more" imply that there were none left and no more were to be made.

Printers

At the turn of the 19th century, Alston Moor possessed a series of printers with ambitious plans. In 1799 John Harrop printed twelve numbers of 'The Alston Miscellany' from April 1799 to March 1800. In 1807 George Boyd, a printer born at Greyfriars in Edinburgh, was resident in the town. In 1810 a company probably run by local man, T. Walton & Co., published 'Lives of the Most Eminent English Poets' by Samuel Johnston in two volumes. Then, from before 1826 until the 1870's, John Pattinson was in business as Alston's printer and bookbinder.

The saw mill

Alston's saw mill was located on the mill race at the end of King's Arms Lane in the Butts. Its first appearance in a trades directory was in 1858, when it was run by the Haldon family, who were also grocers. The Haldons ran the saw mill until about 1890, when Hugh Kearton, a builder, took it over for about ten years. He was followed by Herbert Richardson who, as well as supplying and cutting timber and making carts and wagons, diversified into cutting marble and granite memorials until the 1920's.

The ropery

At the top of the town on the road to Garrigill is a terrace of houses known as 'The Ropery'. From 1829 or before until about 1881 it was a rope making works owned and run by one man, William Boucock from Marston in Lancashire. He neither married to have a son to continue the business, nor does he appear to have had any employees, and in the 1881 census, at the age of 86, he still described himself as a ropemaker. The ropery closed when he retired, or died at his post.

The woollen factory

The late 18th and early 19th centuries saw a great increase in the number of textile factories in Britain, and Alston acquired its own woollen mill. Part of the building still stands in the present day scrapyard beside the River Nent. The factory was built in the first years of the 19th century and advertised for rent in the Carlisle Journal of Saturday 12th June 1802.

> *"TO BE LET - By Private Contract - For such a Term of Years as may be agreed upon, And entered upon immediately. A New Mill, fit for spinning COTTON and FLAX, situated at Aldston in Cumberland. At one end of a very powerful Overfall Water Wheel (supplied with plenty of Water that never freezes in Winter) is a building 31 feet long, and 32 feet wide - Four Rooms and a Garret, each of the above size, At the other end of the Wheel are Erections fit for Preparing, together with several other valuable Conveniences.*
>
> *For further particulars apply to Wm. Todd of Aldston, the Owner, who will let the same.*
>
> *N.B. here are plenty of Labourers of all descriptions to be had, on very reasonable Terms."*

As an aside, one wonders just how true was the claim to *"water that never freezes"*, here on Alston Moor, but the water wheel itself was quite spectacular, 4½ feet wide and 50 feet in diameter.

The ownership changed fairly frequently. In a directory of 1828-1829 Thomas Bentley was a linen manufacturer and William Atkin was a wool spinner, either of whom could have occupied the building, which became a worsted manufactory under Smith, Stobart & Co. in the 1840's, only to be taken over by Robert Walton & Co. in 1848. After Robert Walton's death in 1849 his family carried on the business in his name until it was sold to the Alston Carpet and Woollen Mill Co. Ltd. in the 1860's, who employed eleven carpet makers in 1871, but none of them were local men, most coming from Kendal. The carpet factory was almost defunct by June 1874 when the local newspaper stated that *"most of the machinery is at a stand, nearly the whole of the hands having been paid off"* and that it had had *"a brisk but brief career"*. It had changed hands again by 1876, when, under the new management of the Akerigg Brothers & Co. Ltd., Woollen Manufacturers, twenty-four men, eight women and twenty "journey persons", or casual workers, were employed.

The factory suffered a serious fire in 1878 and it had to be rebuilt by the Akeriggs, William, Joseph and James, who were from Kendal. The factory re-opened and it worked for only a few more years before final closure in the 1880's. The company went into liquidation and all the machinery and equipment was sold off by auction in May 1889. In William Wallace's view, writing in 1886, *"this mill has proved an unfortunate speculation to most of the owners who have had it in possession"*. At the time of the auction, there was a suggestion to turn the factory into a paper mill, but nothing came of it.

Other mineral extraction

Due to the geological structure of the Alston Block, the extraction of several minerals could sometimes be carried out on the same site. For instance at Flowedge, to the south of Alston, zinc and lead were worked concurrently in the 1840's, followed by the extraction of coal.

Apart from lead and silver, there were other extractive industries on Alston Moor that were not so well recorded, for example zinc, iron, a small amount of copper, stone quarrying, coal mining and lime-burning. Then in the twentieth century lead mines and their spoil heaps were re-worked for fluorspar to be used in steel making.

Lime burning

Most of the lime burning in the area was for direct use on the land by the farmers, but for a time there was commercial production. Above Alston on the Bayle Hill road, there used to be 'Jackson's Lime Kilns' that worked before the enclosures of 1820 until about 1875. In that year operations moved to the top of North Loaning to be run by the 'Alston Lime Company'.

The company built two new limekilns and the next year they opened depots in Heaton and Gateshead. It was intended to build two more kilns and in 1880 construction of a tramway was proposed alongside the Blagill road to the coal mine on Mount Hooley, but these plans did not materialise. However, in 1881, 600 yards of the road behind the quarry was re-routed behind the old toll house to allow the expansion of the Coatley Hill quarry workings. The Coatley Hill quarry was soon worked out and the old quarry at Newshield was re-opened where seventeen men were employed. This phase of operations lasted until 1898 when the owner, Thomas Walter Benson, surrendered the lease. A claim for damaged land followed in 1899 which was settled for £75, and the coal mine continued until 1906.

The horse-drawn tramway route from the kilns to the quarries can still be seen along the hillside and the gravity-worked inclined plane that lowered the tipper waggons to the staithes beside the main line is still an obvious feature, with its tunnel under the A686 road to Hexham. In 1891 George Dickinson of Kings Arms Lane in Alston was the "Waggon Braker" at the top of the incline.

The kilns at the top of North Loaning, Alston

Iron mining

Alston Moor is not well known for its iron ore, but overall it produced 2% of Cumberland's total output, the rest was mined in vast quantities around Whitehaven.

In the 1840's, competition in the iron market was fierce. Iron from Glasgow was cheaper than iron produced in the north east of England and in 1845 ironworks on Tyneside started to import Scottish ironstone instead of the ores from nearby Whitby. There seems to have been an 'iron rush' akin to a gold rush at this time, for between 1844 and 1845 iron prices in Glasgow had recovered in a spectacular fashion from 40/- per ton to 120/-. Obviously here was something to capitalise on as soon as possible. Because of this there was a degree of urgency to develop an iron industry in the manor of Alston Moor.

Transport was the key to iron smelting, any potential iron industry on the Moor could not compete without rail transport and Alston Moor had no railways in 1845. Yet even with the absence of railways, during 1845, 205 tons of iron ore were sent from Alston Moor to the railhead at Haydon Bridge. The supply and the demand were there, it was important therefore to get things moving.

Jacob Walton, the lead mining 'adventurer' commemorated by the memorial beside the Town Hall, was instrumental in the development of the iron industry on Alston Moor because he held the iron ore leases and for several years had been exploring the potential for production. The first customers were the Bell Brothers, of the Walker Iron Works in Newcastle, who, in January 1846, were carrying out trials with the Alston ore on Park Fell and later on Killhope. Even though the quality of their sample was found to be "middling", they still wanted to buy it. There was even talk of the construction of an iron foundry down the valley towards Slaggyford, but things went wrong and by 1848 the Bells withdrew and Jacob Walton fell out with his financial partner James Attwood, owner of the Tindale Spelter Works. It was only in the 1850's that the situation revived.

Joseph Paull, Moormaster for the Greenwich Hospital on Alston Moor, produced a report in February 1860 on the *"prospects for the raising of ironstone from personal inspection & information from Mr. Roddam the*

Agent & communicated to the Derwent & Consett Iron Co. Ltd. on the 9th inst."

He listed several sites around the Moor where trials had been carried out. These were at Thorngill, Low Craig, Nattrass, Nest, Brownside, Gill House, Rock Hill, Horse Edge and the Manor House Mine beside the railway station, where the greatest quantity was produced. Paull said, *"The above are those veins containing ironstone in large quantities where the Ironstone Cos. operations have been extended but there are several other veins known to contain that substance."*

The last iron mining venture of any size was the Woodlands mine, on the opposite side of the river from the railway at Alston. On August 4th 1874 the Alston Herald reported,

> *"The prospects of the district, so far as remunerative labour is concerned, are far from encouraging, work being slack. There is still a little being done in the production of ironstone but owing to the heavy item of carriage, not on the railway but to the railway, such operations are of a limited nature. We are glad to see that the proprietors of the Woodlands mine are manifesting more than usual activity. To save the heavy and roundabout conveyance from the mine to the railway station a bridge has been thrown over the Tyne and a line of rails laid, so that the stone can be tipped into the railway trucks. We had the pleasure of seeing the first waggon conveyed over the bridge and new line on the afternoon of Wednesday last (July 29th). This mine which is under the management of Mr. William Phillipson, has done good to the district by keeping a number of men in good work, and we are glad of any indication of permanency, or an extension of operations."*

The mine does not show on the Second Edition Ordnance Survey Map of 1899, so the mine must have closed before then and the railway bridge demolished.

The output of iron ore from Alston Moor for the years 1856 – 1875 is given in the following table:

Year	Tons	Year	Tons
1856	8,089	1864	500
1857	10,113	1867	25

1858	17,094	1869	140
1859	1,871	1870	1,349
1860	1,931	1871	1,863
1861	101	1873	3,032
1862	820	1874	3,029
1863	891	1875	1,150

Public utilities, services and administration

Water supply

The first of the public utilities to arrive in the 19th century was the supply of water, piped to Alston in 1808 at a cost of £200.16s.8d., raised by public subscription. In fact the fund was over subscribed, £203.7s.6d. being the sum donated. A list was published of those people who contributed money, but there were also sixteen men who gave between a half a day and three days labour free of charge.

The water supply ran from a spring on Broadpot Hill, on the Nenthead Road, to four 'pants' or standpipes; one at Town Foot, one at the future site of the Town Hall, another at the Market Cross, and one at Back o' the Burn. However, the area around the Butts did not receive its water supply until later.

The first meeting of Alston with Garrigill Rural District Council was held on 24th December 1894, and in November 1898 it invoked the Public Health Act of 1875, Section 39, which gave, *"powers to provide public necessaries"* (toilets). Two years later, it was reported that the waterworks, including those in the Butts, were *"proceeding"*. This led to an interesting situation that was discussed at the February meeting in 1895;

> *"The* (Sanitary) *Inspector reported that Complaints had been made from the high part of the Town of the short supply of Water caused by residents in the Lower part of the Town allowing their Water Taps to run. ... Resolved ... that the Sanitary Inspector be Instructed to stop the supply of Water going to the lower half of the Town for about half the day, so that the higher part of the Town may have the service of the Water during that part of the day until further notice."*

A group of people in one of the overcrowded back lanes of Alston

Sanitation

Waste disposal was crude to say the least. Minutes of the Rural Sanitary Board Meetings have frequent references to 'nuisances', the like of which we do not suffer today, for example:-

9th July 1881: *"Ordered that the Inspector give notice to Thomas Spark to remove a nuisance on his premises at the Back of the Burn in Alston occasioned by the depositing of offal from his Slaughter House, and in the event of his non compliance with such notice that the Inspector cause him to be summonsed to appear before the Justices at Alston."*

25th July 1891: *"The Inspector of Nuisances having reported that a certain drain passing through certain houses at Nenthead was out of repair and in a condition prejudicial to health; ordered that a new pipe sewer be constructed and made to pass outside the said houses."*

30th March 1895: *"A letter was read signed by the Rev'd. J.E. Page and others complaining of the Deposit of Night Soil and other refuse on the Fairhill and asking that the nuisance may be removed. Ordered that the same being a deposit on private property and out of the jurisdiction of this Council, the Council cannot see their way to interfere with it."*

By 1900 sewers were being laid, but connection was not automatic, it had to be applied for, so presumably the problems of 'nuisances' and 'night soil' continued for a while.

Work in progress at one of Alston's street lamps

Gas

Alston's Gas Works were erected in 1843, some twenty-five years later than the county town of Carlisle, and the town was first lit in the May of that year. Alston was described in the 1859 trades directory as *"well lighted"*.

The works were the property of a joint stock company and its manager was described as a 'Gas Maker' in the early years.

Managers of the works were entitled to sell the by-product of coke to the public a perquisite that continued until the conversion to LPG in 1960. For the first twenty years, the Manager was Ralph Smith, followed by William Walton, then Joseph Pickering for another twenty to twenty five years.

In November 1871 the Inspectors for Lighting the Town of Alston had to deal with a gas price increase. Their solution was that they *"Ordered that owing to an increase being made in the price of Gas the Street Lamps in future be extinguished immediately after eleven o'clock each night but not before, and in consideration of which the Gas Co. will not increase the rate of charge for Gas"*.

The railway

In late 1852, the Newcastle and Carlisle Railway completed Alston's railway link to the outside world. This put an end to the short-lived coach services which had started in 1829, and was seen by some to be an aid to the drift of people away from Alston Moor.

When the first train ran in 1852 the event was described by Joseph Pearson, the local postman:

"January 5th. The long expected day for opening the Alston Branch of Railway arrived, the New Band left Alston at 7 o'clock for the terminus where a truck was prepared, it was drawn by a horse to Gilderdale where the Alston Engine were waiting their arrival., they then proceeded to Lambley where a party of the Railway Co. met them, the Band played at intervals all the way to Alston where many people with flags and roars of cannon met the arrival of the first Locomotive Engine that ever came to Alston. The Train consisted of the engine and tender, two passenger Carriages, a low truck with the Band and last 10 waggons of Coals, the Coals were given to the Poor by 10 horses and carts, the horses had rosetts at each ear with ribands. (the first fruits of a Railway, Charity Coals for the poor) the 10 Carts of Coals were preceeded by the Band to the Lockup, where the Band stood in front till the Coals were tip't or emptied, then the carts returned for more.

When the Railway was opened the Engine returned for more waggons of Coals and Slates. Some boys from Slaggyford got upon a truck loaded with slates and when the train arrived at Lowbyre owing to the crowd of people, the speed was slackened so as to cause a jerk and three of the boys fell off the truck of slates, one got his arm much hurt by the wheel taking off a part of skin and flesh, another Joseph Teasdale got both his feet crushed as to cause amputation necessary, the next morning he died in consequence Verdict Accidental death, no one being to blame, but the carelessness of the suffering party."

The railway was opened for paying passengers from Lambley to Alston on Friday 21st May. The first station master was William Little, succeeded in the late 1870's by Joseph Walton. Walton was only 25 years old in 1881 and he remained in post until about the turn of the century.

The railway had been planned with the aim of transporting lead away from the Moor, but by 1852 that industry was already in decline. However, it did a massive trade in transporting limestone and roadstone from the quarries adjacent to the station; the railway company had to lay four extra sidings capable of holding 150 wagons to cope with the traffic.

The railway station ca.1900

The police station

In the early years of the century, law had been administered by elected constables, and the 'Alston Moor Association' had been established in 1807 for apprehending law-breakers, but this nationally ad hoc approach was not satisfactory, and the government decided to do something. In 1847, as a belated response to an Act of Parliament of 1843, *"For the Appointment and Payment of Parish Constables"*, Justices of the Peace for the various wards of Cumberland petitioned for the provision of town Lock-ups. These were not to be prisons, but simply holding cells for "persons not yet committed to trial", and the longest that these persons could be held was forty-eight hours, before conveyance to Carlisle. Alston's petition was signed by Rev. Hugh Salvin, Chairman, C.W.G. Howard, Thomas Wilson, W. Marshall, and William ...thorpe. Tenders for the building contract were submitted in 1847, and the Lock-up was built at Townhead soon afterwards and opened on 4th May 1850.

Joseph Pearson the postman/diarist recorded that on May 1st the new constable arrived at Alston and entered on duty on Saturday May 4th. Then on May 5th *"About 1 o'clock in the morning A travelling Tinker put into Lock up being the first admitted into that Elegent Edifice"*.

The building had three cells and accommodation for one Inspector. Quotations for fire insurance in 1857 show that the value of Alston's Lock-up was £700, and by 1862 its value had increased to £862.10s.11d., by which time Lock-ups were referred to as Police Stations.

The detainees had to be fed, but the fare was basic and the same for men and women: Breakfast, one pint of milk porridge; Dinner, one pound weight of bread and two ounces of country cheese; Supper one pint of milk porridge.

The Town Hall

For thirty years or so, between about 1840 and 1870, there was a huge amount of public building work carried out on Alston Moor. In addition to the new police station, there were churches, chapels, schools, the railway station, the gas works, and Alston Moor acquired its own Town - not village - Hall.

The Town Hall is Alston's bit of neo-Gothic. Designed by A.B. Higham, the foundation stone was laid on 15th July 1857 by Alston Moor's most famous son, Hugh Lee Pattinson. The construction, on a site adjacent to the vicarage given by the Greenwich Hospital, was funded by public subscription. The cheapest builder's estimate of £1,630 was accepted but the actual cost, including the Savings Bank, was £2,199.13s.7d. Accommodation included a Public Hall, a Gentlemen's Reading Room, the Mechanics Institute, a Library, and a meeting room for the Poor Law Guardians.

The Alston Savings Bank helped with the funding and in return obtained the adjoining site on which to build their bank in a matching style. The result was that the bank appeared to be a part of the Town Hall, as indeed it is now.

The Town Hall was and still is the location for most of the town's entertainment. From the Alston Herald of the 5th December 1874 there was marvellous entertainment to be had in the approach to Christmas, and what a show it was!

Monuments

Other than War Memorials, Alston Moor has only two public monuments. One is the present Market Cross which was erected in 1883. The other is a monument sited near to the Town Hall dedicated to a local mine owner and agent Jacob Walton, who died in 1863. He was described as *"an extensive mining proprietor of considerable ability"*, and at his funeral all shops were shut as a mark of respect. The monument was removed in the 1960's to make way for a road improvement scheme at Townfoot, and it was not replaced until 2004.

The Market Place was originally owned by the Greenwich Hospital where a cross was erected in 1765, presumably to replace the one on the site where John Wesley preached in 1748, with money from the Right Honourable Sir William Stephenson, Bart., a native of Alston who had become Lord Mayor of London in 1764. 160 years later Alston produced another Lord Mayor, this time of Newcastle, when in the 1920's Mr. R.H. Millican was elected.

---------------oo0O0oo---------------

TOWN HALL ALSTON

Friday and Saturday December 11 and 12 1874
*The stage will be beautifully fitted up for the occasion. The room
will be perfumed by Rimmel's Apparatus.*
*Admission – First Class, 2s.; Second, 1s.; Third, 6d.; Family
tickets admitting Five to first class, 8s.*
Tickets to be had at the usual places in the town.
Doors open at 7.30. Wonders commence at 8. Carriages at 10.
Visit of the well-known and World Renowned Professor

CRISTO

*The Greatest Organophonic VENTRILOQUIST ever known,
Hindoo Illusionist and Anti-Spiritualist, will have the honour of
presenting his Extraordinary Entertainment, entitled*

A WORLD OF SPIRITS

*As given by him with the most brilliant success in London, and
nearly all the principal cities of the world, before the most fashionable
audiences ever assembled together. See patrons names.*
*The grand secrets of the ancient Egyptian Magicians, and the
startling wonders of the Modern Spiritualists fully explained, and
learned by him in Japan, China, Hindostan, and Arabia, in which
countries he was known as*

THE MAN OF WONDER

or Music Throat Man
Solo Pianiste..........................Miss Marian Hill
Agent in Advance.....................Sam Varder
Sole Proprietor........................Professor Cristo from Quebec.

---------------oo0O0oo---------------

The Alston Mountain Rifles

The Crimean War formally ended with the Treaty of Paris in March 1856 and Alston Moor celebrated on May 29th with a fair, *"a fine day, public rejoicing in honour of the peace with all Europe"*, with three triumphal arches and tea for four or five hundred in the infant school, followed by fireworks at night. But the fear of war touched Alston Moor again when relations between Britain and France quickly deteriorated to the point that on the 1st July 1859 Parliament announced the formation of volunteer corps (the forerunners of the Territorial Army) up and down the country to assist the regular army.

By February 1860 Cumberland had eleven corps, of which the men of Alston Moor made up the 6th Corps (Alston) Rifle Volunteers, also known as the Alston Mountain Rifles, or the Alston Mountaineers. The regiment was the sixth of eight raised in Cumberland and its distinctive identity lasted twenty-one years until 1881, when it became a volunteer battalion of the Border Regiment.

The Mountain Rifles mustered in their grey uniforms on 1st June 1860, and marched to the Town Hall where they were enrolled. To show that they meant business, the volunteers were issued with Enfield musket rifles. The first drill had been held in Alston Town Hall on February 22nd with instructor Colour-Sergeant Carruthers of the Cumberland and Westmorland Militia, but it was not until the early summer that the volunteers had been drilled sufficiently to appear in public. The "Carlisle Patriot" of 9th June, 1860 reported the muster, abbreviated as follows:

ALSTON – The highest market town has not been the lowest in its own estimation during the last week – and justly. It has the heart to conceive great things and the nerve to carry them out.

On Friday, the 1st June a scene of considerable interest presented itself to the inhabitants of this comparatively secluded district. The Alston Mountaineer Rifle Volunteers, forming the 6th. Cumberland Corps, made their debut and appeared for the first time in full regimental costume. The uniform is an exceedingly neat one, being of a light grey colour, the cloth of which it is made being composed of the natural wool of the sheep – black and white. Shortly after noon the members assembled on the parade ground at the Tyne Willows near the town where the corps, after being put through several military evolutions by their drill instructor, formed "fours-right" and marched to the Town Hall, attended by the Garrigill band, where they were enrolled. At four o'clock p.m. the members of the corps dined together at the Golden Lion Inn, after which a second drill took place, and then the corps marched through the town accompanied by the band, and afterwards dismissed.

The Corps was very popular with the people, whose support was demonstrated by the results of a fund-raising bazaar *"for the benefit of the Riflemen"* held at the Town Hall on Thursday 26th September 1862. £263.3s.2d. was raised on the day and by 1st October the amount had risen to £300!

The Volunteers soon established a routine of regular events. The first drill of season was held in February or March, probably according to the weather. Then twice-weekly drills were held on Wednesdays and Fridays. A New Year's Day Prize Shoot was held at Lovelady Shield, the home of solicitor Joseph Dickinson. The month of June saw the Cumberland and Westmorland Rifle Association Annual Competition held at different venues around the county, as was the Cumberland Challenge Cup held each August. There was the Annual Review at Carlisle, and, back at Alston in October, the Annual Prize Shoot was held at the home shooting range, which was first at Skellgill then after April 1876 at Rotherhope, or Rodderup as it was known until quite recent times. There were also occasional 'friendly' shooting matches with other corps in the north, for example at Carlisle, Brampton, Whitehaven and Barnard Castle. The shooting distances were 300, 500 and 700 yards.

All the shooting competitions were reported in detail in the 'Alston Herald', including the prize lists. In 1876 at the Prize Shooting at the Skelgill range on New Year's Day sixty-four volunteers shot for prizes donated by the local community, and every participant was awarded a prize, ranging from a teapot to an armchair, from a shirt to ½ ton of coal, or to two rabbits. There was also a special gift for Private John Edgar who was seriously ill. Sadly, Private Edgar did not recover and his funeral was held on the 29th January when he was buried with military honours. He was twenty-one years old.

In January 1876 new physical qualifications for volunteers were announced. No one under 5ft. 3in., or with a chest measuring less than thirty-two inches would be accepted. Also, *"When a corps of rifle volunteers is permitted to adopt a scarlet tunic or patrol jacket, the facings must be similar to those of the County militia"*. At the AGM in March 1877, *"Capt. Dickinson intimated that it was intended during the spring to have the men re-clothed as many of the uniforms were worn out"*, and by July, *"The corps has lately been partially re-clothed and the men now wear the new battalion tunic. They have also obtained a new band, their own having been recently broken up; they have been joined by members of the Garrigill band"*.

Even thought the Alston Mountaineers were the second smallest corps, they had some riflemen of note. On 19th July 1879 'The Herald' reported on "THE WIMBLEDON MEETING - SUCCESS OF ALSTON MARKSMEN", where Lieutenants Dickinson and Akerigg received £12 and a badge from the National Rifle Association.

After twenty years of having its distinctive title, the 6th Corps (Alston) Rifle Volunteers, the Alston Mountain Rifles, or the Alston Mountaineers, came to an end on 16th March 1880 when the eight sub-units of the Cumberland volunteers were consolidated in 1st Cumberland Rifle Volunteers and, officially at least, "The Alston Mountaineers" became known simply and less romantically as "J Company". The next year, on 1st July 1881 the corps became a Volunteer Battalion of the Border Regiment.

In the 1998 edition of 'A History of Alston Moor' I wrote, *"Their banner still hangs (in a sorry state) in St. Augustine's Church"*. I am happy to say that the banner is now in the care of the Border Regiment Museum in Carlisle Castle, which also holds a belt buckle of the Corps. A ceremonial sword, photos of a shako badge and two volunteers in uniform, and bullets found by a local resident at the Rodderup Fell Range are in the Alston Moor Historical Society Archives.

Volunteers of the Alston Mountain Rifles photographed in the 1870's

Chartism

Oddly enough, Chartism features slightly in Alston's history. In her Ph.D. thesis, 'Radical Politics in Carlisle 1790-1850', June C.F. Barnes revealed in 1981, that Dr. Taylor, a revolutionary from Ayrshire and one of the movement's leaders, came to Alston and held secret meetings here. An informer told the Moormaster, who in turn told John Grey at Dilston, the

Receiver for the Greenwich Hospital in the north. Alston had been chosen as a central point for the movement in the area to gain support from Kendal, Carlisle and Newcastle. Taylor boasted of many thousands of adherents and it was planned to attack Newcastle first. A man called Hanson was to take the petition and People's Charter to Alston and West Cumberland. Chartism clearly shocked Grey, so he was happy to report a month later that Dr. Taylor was in Carlisle prison and the 'Lawless crew' had been dispersed.

"On November 18th, a fortnight after the Newport rising (of 1839 when the army shot at the mob leaving several people dead), *the Carlisle police caught up with Dr. Taylor to execute the warrant against him in the remote fellside village of Melmerby, between Penrith and Alston. There, in company with Cardo, the London shoemaker, he was either lying low following Newport, or perhaps aiming to organise the lead miners in the Alston area for another attempt at a rising."*

Emigration

There was a long economic slump from 1810 to 1825, mainly as a result of the Napoleonic Wars and their aftermath. Because of this, the government abandoned its former attitude of opposition to emigration and instead began to give financial aid. In 1818 the 'Jason', a *"square sterned brigantine"* with two masts and a single deck, set sail from Whitehaven for Upper Canada, or Ontario as we now know it. One hundred and ten men, women and children, including families from of Alston Moor, landed at Quebec on 19th September to start their new lives. William, John and Isaac Dixon, Thomas and Robert Milburn, Joseph John and George Lee, John and Robert Walton, Walton Wilson, and John Smith, all from Alston Moor, were among those who left their families behind in Port Hope, Ontario, and travelled north to locate their land grants. They built shanties in Smith Township to live in during winter, before claiming their grants in spring, and returning to collect their families.

The 1830's saw the lowest lead prices for fifty years. This led to a great deal of unemployment, and most of the small independent mining companies went out of business. Public works that included the construction of the turnpike roads and walling for the enclosures, which had been instigated by the Greenwich Hospital and the London Lead Company in the 1820's, absorbed some of the unemployed. However there was a flow of labour away to the nearest industrial centres, and in addition further schemes were set up for the emigration of 'surplus labour', especially to North America.

The Poor Law Commission found that between 1831 and 1832, 2,000 people had left Alston Moor, many for Upper Canada. Emigration was not, however, confined to unemployed miners with their families. A list of those who left Alston Moor in 1832 includes single women, and widows with their children. Nor was this emigration only from Alston Moor. By 1839 it was thought that 1,200,000 British citizens had taken up residence in North America.

Yet it was during this period of economic depression that Hugh Lee Pattinson, an Alston man talented in several fields, made his name in 1829 by inventing and patenting a process of cupellation for economically de-silvering lead. His reward from the London Lead Company was £16,000.

The lead industry recovered but, in spite of the optimism and civic pride evinced by the construction of new public buildings, the second half of the 19th century was a period of sharpening decline for Alston Moor. The lead industry, used to ups and downs, was in terminal decline during the last quarter of the century, lead mines were being worked out, and imported lead provided cheaper alternative supplies, which led to falling prices at home. In 1882, after nearly 200 years on Alston Moor, the London Lead Company sold out to Cameron, Swan & Company of Newcastle, who owned the Nenthead and Tynedale Lead and Zinc Company. This company's interest lasted only fourteen years, before it in turn sold out to the Vieille Montagne Zinc Company of Belgium in 1896.

This decline in the industry forced people to move away to search for work. The extent of migration was reflected in the population census figures, which, from a peak of 6,858 in 1831, with two exceptions, continued steadily downwards for the next 150 years. The first exception when the downward trend was temporarily reversed was in 1851 when the presence of several hundred railway navvies boosted the population. The second occasion was in the following century, when the census of 1921 showed a possible post war baby boom.

In common with most parishes in the country, Alston Moor had its own emigration scheme. *"An Account of Receipts and Disbursements by the Committee respecting the Emigration to Upper Canada, of Poor Persons belonging to the Parish of Alston Moor, in the Year 1832"*, showed that £310.16s. had been raised to assist twenty-four households and individuals, making a total of 124 people, to emigrate to Upper Canada, the area around Toronto towards the Great Lakes. £200 of the overall sum came from the Greenwich Hospital, £25 from the London Lead Company and the rest was donated by local individuals. A disbursement item of £5.3s.6d was described as "Various Expenses in removing the Emigrants to the Sea Coast &c, &c."

Prospective emigrants were obviously means tested, for example one widow received £3 while another received £4, and one family of six received £2, while another family of six received £5.

Twenty years later emigration was still happening. Joseph Pearson, a postman of Alston, kept a diary of local events in which he also recorded emigrants from Alston Moor between 1849 and 1856, and people from Weardale and Allendale who passed through the town on their way to their port of emigration at Liverpool. In 1851 he recorded the progress of one man, William Thompson.

On July 18th William Thompson junior, a thirty-one year old gardener whose father owned and ran the Lowbyer Nursery Gardens, left Alston for Liverpool on his way to North America. On July 19th he went on board the Kalamazoo, a vessel of 1,000 tons with three masts, carrying about 200 passengers from Liverpool for New York which was due to sail on Monday the 21st. The food allowance on board ship for one week was 2½lb biscuit, 1lb wheat flour, 5lb oatmeal, 2lb rice, ½lb sugar, ½lb molasses, 2oz. tea and 21 quarts (42 pints) of water.

Thompson landed at New York on September 1st after six weeks and two days at sea. From there he went on to Philadelphia where he arrived on September 5th. His letter posted on the 8th arrived at Alston on September 22nd.

At the turn of the 20th century the future looked bleak for Alston Moor; its staple industry was vanishing, there were no alternatives of a similar scale to expand and take up the workforce, and the area was too remote to attract new industries.

THE TWENTIETH CENTURY

Mining and quarrying

Lead, zinc and fluorspar

Although the paternal London Lead Company had gone, and with it the security that people had known for 150 years, in the lead mines there was still a glimmer of hope. The Vieille Montagne Company was extracting zinc ore that had been untouched for many years and continued to do so until 1948, albeit with a more mechanised system, and on a reduced scale of manpower. The Vieille Montagne, on its acquisition of the leases, exported all the concentrates for smelting to its home country of Belgium, transporting them by road to the railhead at Alston, using 'road trains' hauled by two traction engines.

The company demolished the old public wash house and clock tower in Nenthead in 1908, and built a new dressing plant in 1909 of the most up-to-date type powered by electricity. Further purchases of leases in 1914 led to the acquisition of the Brownley Hill and Nentsberry mines, the latter from the Nentsberry Mining Co., which had worked Nentsberry Haggs Mine.

After the First World War the Vielle Montagne stared up again and straight away it was faced with a shortage of miners, so as well as processing all the new ore that could be mined, the company additionally blended wastes reprocessed from the old waste heaps. However, the enterprise was not a success, some levels were closed in 1918 and two hundred miners were laid off. In the following year the last level closed and a further fifty men became unemployed. The Vieille Montagne ceased operating in Nenthead in 1921.

In the period between the wars, when Amos Treloar was manager for the Vieille Montagne, only three lead mines were worked, which all belonged to that company:- Brownley Hill, which was worked briefly in 1936; Haggs Bank Mine at Nentsberry, which produced unprecedented tonnages of very rich ore between 1926 and 1938, and the Rotherhope Fell Mine. The latter mine had been purchased by the Vieille Montagne from the Rotherhope Fell Mining Company in 1900, and it was worked until closure in 1930. Then Rotherhope was reopened in 1935 and continued with a large output of high grade ore and fluorspar throughout the Second World War, but it became exhausted soon afterwards, closing in 1948.

During both wars many mines were re-opened and explored for minerals but this lasted only for the duration. At Nenthead, the waste heaps were reworked for lead by the Ministry of Supply during the Second World War, and the plant was dismantled soon afterwards. Major parts of Nenthead smelt mill were reasonably intact until it was dismantled in the late 1960's to retrieve the building materials.

Nenthead before 1904.
A tramway runs along the top of the waste heaps in the middle of the picture.

The mine leases were taken over by the Anglo Austral Co. of Avonmouth in 1948. That year the new company closed Rotherhope mine, but reopened Nentsberry Haggs in 1950, which it worked for two years before the mine was finally closed in 1952.

Umber

Since at least 1829 ochre, or umber, had been obtained from Gilderdale for local use in yellow and red paints, but its first commercial exploitation had not been until the 1890's. In the 1894 Directory, the Cumberland Umber Company, later the Whitlow Fell Umber Company, worked an old lead mine in Gilderdale for umber to be used in paint manufacture, but the enterprise failed in the early 1900's, possibly because of the inaccessibility of the site. The Horse Edge vein in Gilderdale was worked again during the First World War, then trench-worked in 1942 for the Ministry of Supply and in an industrial survey of 1951 it was thought to be worth working again at some time in the future.

Roadstone and railway ballast

The 'Alston and Nentforce Limestone Quarry Company' probably started operation about 1890, for the first mention in a trades directory from 1894 records that James Polglase of Hundy House on Front Street in Alston was the manager and C.W. Harrison was the secretary. In 1901 James Emmerson, of Townhead, Alston, was the manager and Walter Cecil Reid the secretary of the company whose registered office was at 1, St. Nicholas Buildings, Newcastle-on-Tyne.

The quarry is right next to the railway station and across the Hexham road in another quarry alongside the River Nent that reaches past the Nent Force waterfall. The company struggled to survive for many years, with the North Eastern Railway as its main customer for railway ballast and local authorities for roadstone, before finally succeeding, by which time its quarrying operations were away from Alston Moor. In the later years of the 1930's a stocktaking exercise was carried out which revealed that the company held land at Alston and buildings and land at various locations in the Tyne valley. In terms of contracts, in 1937 the company had contracts at West Rainton, South Biddick, Blaydon and Whickham.

In April 1939 as 'Alston Limestone Company Ltd.' it was sold to Amalgamated Roadstone Corporation Ltd. and was associated with Alston in name only. The company, thenceforward known as ALCO, prospered greatly. In 1977 it was purchased by the Thomas Tilling Group, who owned TILCON. Ultimately, ALCO's parent company was Anglo American PLC that purchased Tarmac in 2000. Throughout this time the Alston Limestone Company remained an independent subsidiary company, trading independently with its own board of directors and registered as a separate limited company at Companies House. In the year ending 31st December 2005, ALCO's turnover was £12.2m.

STATEMENT.

10, Neville Street,

Newcastle-on-Tyne,

Messrs: the
Rural Dist: Council,
Haltwhistle.

10th Nov: 1906

Dr. to the Alston & Nentforce Limestone Quarry Co.

1906.

					£	s	d
Oct:	14	To a/c. Rendered			34	1	4
"	22	" " "			8	2	6
				£	42	3	10

Received Cheque
10th Nov 1906.
pp. The Alston & Nentforce
Limestone Co
B.R.

With thanks.

Statement from the Alston and Nentforce Limestone Quarry Co. Ltd., 1906

Lime burning

During the economic depression of the 1930's, Alston was a particularly distressed area. The lead and zinc were almost completely worked out and there was no industry to replace it. Long queues of unemployed men waited outside the post office to receive their 17/- per week benefit. This sight particularly grieved Alston's vicar, Rev. Norman A. Walton. Rev. Walton had a knowledgeable interest in geology and instigated experiments, possibly at Shap, to discover the purity of the local lime and it was found to be 78%. That of Shap was 72%, so Alston could supply something for which there was a demand.

The next step was to form a company. Rev. Walton wanted the proposed limeworks to be a community concern, so he appealed for people to become company members and to subscribe funds to get the enterprise started. Few citizens of Alston Moor answered the call, but nevertheless a committee was formed and the company was incorporated on 23rd September 1937, to become 'Walton's Alston Lime and Coal Company Limited': It was named "Walton's" because the Reverend and his wife were by far the major parties and also to distinguish this company from the Alston Limestone Company.

The bases chosen for the proposed operations were the old limekilns at the top of North Loaning that had not been used since the First World War and were in a very poor state of repair, the adjacent Newshield limestone quarries and the nearby Blagill Colliery, abandoned by the Alston and Nentforce Limestone Company in 1906.

Operations began in autumn 1937. Office space was obtained in the Market Place and a small workforce was employed whose first job was to rebuild and repair the kilns and raise their height. About twelve men were to be employed at the quarry itself.

Rev. Walton went to the Glasgow Exhibition of 1938, and met agricultural representatives who told him that they would indeed be interested in buying Alston's lime. As for industrial use, the purer the lime, the greater the demand for it. The Scottish contracts started with a lot of lime going by road to Scotland. A lot of lime was also sold to arable farmers in County Durham and to local farmers who had previously burnt their own before the war. The effect on Alston was that the dole queue shrank as around two dozen men went back to work.

An accountant from Haltwhistle was appointed and the company agents, Clark Taylor, also from Haltwhistle, helped tremendously to sell the lime, bringing customers to Alston. Later on they probably invested money in the company.

After the War the limeworks did not thrive, despite assistance from the Ministry of Agriculture they "went back". Rev. Walton had retired at the end of the war at the age of seventy-seven and the works closed about 1959 when the quarry became exhausted. The quarry face was right next to a public road and could be worked no longer.

The lime kilns were demolished, the site was landscaped and the Newshield quarry became a landfill site. The railway trackbed can still be seen plainly as well as the Coatlith Hill quarry face, but they are on private land with no rights of way.

Coal mining

There is another form of mining that has received little mention in any documents throughout the ages, this is the local coal industry. William Wallace wrote in 1890 that at one time Alston was supplied with coal from the head of Gilderdale, but offers no further information. The inventory of James, Earl of Derwentwater, in 1723 refers to a colliery on Hartside Fell, rented by Henry Stephenson at £10.5s. per year. There is also a lot of evidence around Alston Moor of shallow seams of coal being worked near the surface to supply the farmers' field lime kilns, but other than this there is nothing to go on.

The coal field of Alston Moor is different from most others in that the coal is a scarce, high quality semi-anthracite coal used mainly in solid fuel appliances. After a public inquiry in September 1986, followed by the subsequent report, the possibility of open-cast mining, backed by Norwest Holst, on the Mount Hooley hillside from Alston to Blagill was examined and rejected, mainly because of its claimed doubtful viability and the fact that Alston Moor is part of the North Pennines Area of Outstanding Natural Beauty. At the time the debate caused a lot of ill feeling when real jobs in the local coal industry were lost to the promise of jobs in tourism. The opponents of the scheme were accused of being *"tea and bun merchants"* and *"hippies"*.

In the assessment of Cumbria's coal industry by Cumbria County Council in 1988, four mines were reported to be working in the Alston and South Tynedale area, employing a total of between fifty and sixty people. In Northumberland, but still in the Alston catchment area, they were owned and worked mainly by people of Alston Moor and were regarded as being part of the locality, there were Ayle and Tows Bank, which closed in 1995, and the two on Alston Moor were Clarghyll, which was established in 1940, and Blagill, which started in 1986 and closed a few years later. Flow Edge Mine, off the Garrigill road, had been in operation since the 1940's, but it closed in spring 1987. Although this closure was thought to be temporary in 1988, the pit has been lying idle ever since. On one occasion, when the pit was re-opened after a long lay-off, a delivery of coal was made by lorry in record time to the amazement of customers. But the truth was that a heap of good coal had been found just inside the old blocked up mine entrance. Ayle, the last working pit, closed in 2006.

Garrigill Fuse Company

The Garrigill Fuse Company, owned by John Hall of Windy Hall, supplied lead and black powder fuses to Greenside Mine in the Lake District as early as 1856. The factory was situated in Crossgill near Garrigill and used water-powered machines to make metallic fuses for blasting, but little is known about this enterprise. It was last heard of in 1904 when 'Low Crossgill Fuse Factory' was leased, as it had been for many years, to Wallace Millican of Crossgill House and others.

War again

During the Boer War, men of the area enlisted at the Town Hall, and were photographed in uniform both there and outside the Post Office with their horses, but no information is known of the men themselves.

It would appear from photographs that in the early years of the 19th century, Alston Moor was used much as the Otterburn Range in Northumberland is today, or the Warcop Range in Cumbria, for military exercises. For instance there is a photograph of an artillery division crossing the Brewery bridge in 1907, complete with spiked helmets, and in June 1911 an army Medical Corps with horse-drawn ambulances arrived on

Alston Moor to carry out exercises. Preceded by bugles and drums, the 'Medics' marched past the Old Brewery and through Alston to pitch camp for the night on Middle Fell above Farnberry.

Men about to set off for South Africa

Medical Corps on manoeuvres above Farnberry

In common with every other community in Britain, Alston Moor made its human contribution to the Great War. Then, on September 4th 1922, the War Memorial at Alston was unveiled, with the rare inclusion of a woman's name in the Roll of Honour.

Alston War Memorial

Alice Renwick was born in 1890 and lived first at Dorthgill, several miles south of Garrigill, the family moved and in 1901 they were living at Physic Hall, just outside Alston. She joined the Women's Army Auxiliary Corps with the regimental number 5169 and the rank of 'Worker', to become one of 57,000 women at home and overseas. Alice went on overseas service sometime in 1916 and survived the war to return home and to be awarded a Victory medal and a British Empire medal. But tragically Alice died in Newcastle sometime between October and December 1918, probably because of the Spanish flu pandemic that was raging at the time, killing millions.

A serviceman commemorated both on the memorial and in St. Augustine's Church is Lieutenant Nowell Oxland of the 6th Battalion of the Border Regiment, killed at Gallipoli on 9th August 1915. He was the son of Rev. W. Oxland R.N., B.A., vicar at Alston from 1902 until 1917, and attended Worcester College, Oxford. Nowell was one of the war poets;

his poem 'Outward Bound' was published in 'The Times' the year that he died. His body was buried at Green Hill Cemetery in France. At St. Augustine's Church there are two full length portraits of him, commissioned by his parents, one each side of the altar, with Nowell depicted as a knight in armour. Each portrait has a halo.

Eighty-eight men and one woman with Alston Moor connections died in the First World War and twenty-seven men died in the Second World War; they are commemorated on eight memorials on Alston Moor. There are only four war graves, one from 1918 and another from 1946 in Alston cemetery, and two from 1918 in Nenthead.

During the Second World War Alston Moor had the uncommon, if not unique, distinction of possessing a mounted Home Guard division. The unit drew the attention of a national illustrated magazine that put the area on the Home Front map when it published photographs of the Home Guard on horseback.

The 'Mounties', the mounted Home Guard of Alston Moor

On a lighter note, from May 1943 to May 1945 the Observation Corps met in the Turks Head Hotel in a room hired for 8/- per week. Thankfully the harsher realities of war did not reach Alston and the meetings were more social events than military ones.

The foundry

The Second World War saw the establishment of a large scale industry without precedent on Alston Moor - steel making. An article in a wartime edition of the 'Production and Engineering Bulletin' was entitled, 'Shepherds Who Make Steel', which the editors were *"proud to publish"*. This described the establishment of the works in Alston with a labour force of 54% women and 46% men and boys, and the setting and achieving of a target for the manufacture of mortar-bomb cases, in spite of teething difficulties with plant. One week the target for production was 20,000 shells, which meant finishing two bombs per minute, twenty-four hours a day for seven days. The heat in the building was tremendous, the manager wrote, *"In between casts the women went outside and lay down on the ground, absolutely overcome; but never once refused to be on the spot when the next cast was ready"*. A problem occurred one day when a furnace burst. *"This looked the last straw. One of the furnace men said he would try to repair it and he wrapped himself up in asbestos and wet sacking, and stood up to a furnace which only a few moments before had poured steel at a temperature of 1,650 degrees C. He made the repair and just as he finished he collapsed. We carried him outside and got the furnace going again"*. The article did not say what happened later to this hero, presumably he recovered.

An information panel prepared for an exhibition at the Samuel King's School at Alston in 1977 gave the brief history of the foundry to that time.

"The Alston Foundry Co. Ltd. was first formed in 1940 as a subsidiary company of 'The Steel Co. Ltd.' based at Sunderland. (Later to become Cole's Cranes). *The original building had been used as a woollen mill and a crushing plant for the quarry situated at the rear of the present building. The foundry was set up at Alston with the installation of two Bessemer Convertors and production commenced, initially casting 3" mortar-bomb casings followed by chain links for the Admiralty. Government policy at that time was to*

*move manufacturing industries as far inland as possible, away from
the threat of German aircraft bombing coastal ports.*

*The foundry continued in this vein until the end of the war in
1945 when closure seemed imminent. The Cumberland County
Council and the local councils got together and approached Mr. Eric
Steel, the then chairman of the 'Steel Group' in Sunderland in an
effort to keep the foundry open as a going concern manufacturing
commercial castings. In 1946 Alston Foundry Co. commenced
production chiefly for the mining industry and prospered until 1952
when the government cut back in the mechanisation of the mines.*

*The period 1952 to 1955 saw a programme of building up a
service to other industries. At this time an electric arc furnace was
installed which in turn meant a new supply line from Penrith over
the moors to Alston. Also during this time the foundry began
experiments with new moulding techniques with an air-set resin
imported from Western Germany, which today is known throughout
the industry as the Shaw Process. Technical representatives were
engaged and sent out to cover the whole of the country and the
company prospered.*

*In 1971 the company joined the Weir Group of Glasgow
Foundries Division and so became one of the five foundries in the
division. A major project started in 1974 with alterations to the
existing building, new plant and machinery being installed to equip
us with modern techniques. The company are also at present
constructing a new dressing shop from which full production is
expected in 1979."*

In spite of this optimism, reverses set in and collapse came suddenly,
for in October 1979, workers received a notice of closure from the
Managing Director, Frank Allinson. The foundry had employed up to 200
workers, and when it closed in 1980, a workforce of 124 was laid off, taking
Alston's unemployment rate from 8.9% to more than 25%. The premises
were reopened by Frank Allinson as 'Falmech', and operated for several
years before closing again in 1989.

Public transport

An industrial survey of Cumberland in 1951 stated that, *"No outline of the transport facilities of the county would be complete without reference to the most easterly part centring on the small market town of Alston. This lies on the attractive but by no means always easy route, A686, linking Penrith with the Tyne Corridor route near Haydon Bridge. Steepness of gradients, particularly at Hartside where the road descends from the Alston Block to the Eden Valley, limits the use of this road by commercial vehicles and much of the traffic is made up of private vehicles"*.

Average numbers of vehicles passing census points per day in 1931 were 652, in 1935, 702, and in 1938, 818. A survey in 1997 showed that there were 2,200 vehicles passing through Alston each day, ten per cent of which were heavy goods lorries.

The bus service to Alston Moor in 1951 was run by Ribble Motor Services Ltd. Today the few remaining services are operated by the Stagecoach bus company and Wrights Brothers of Nenthead, which is a proudly independent concern, started by George Wright in 1919 with a Model T Ford and still going strong with a fleet of coaches and another base in Newcastle.

When the railway closed in 1976, one of the conditions for closure was that an equivalent bus service would be guaranteed. Intending rail passengers had to travel to Haltwhistle to reach the world beyond. In 1948 there were six trains outward and five trains inward per day, with an extra 'late night' service each way on Saturday. The railway survived the Beeching axe of the 1960's because of social need during winter and hung on throughout several threats of closure until May 1976, when the axe finally fell. Now the first two and a half miles of the trackbed are occupied by the narrow gauge South Tynedale Railway, which attracts many thousands of visitors each year.

T 2468 (HD)

BRITISH RAILWAYS

In conjunction with the
Ramblers Association
(Northern Area)

Conducted Rambles from
Lambley, Slaggyford and Alston
(For routes see over)

*RAMBLES AVAILABLE FOR INDIVIDUALS
AS WELL AS ORGANISED PARTIES*
(Leaders provided)

Special Ramblers Excursion

By Diesel Train to

Haltwhistle, Featherstone Park,
Coanwood, Lambley,
Slaggyford and Alston

SUNDAY 23rd APRIL 1961

OUTWARD	Second Class Return Fares						RETURN	
	Halt-whistle	Feather-stone Park	Coan-wood	Lamb-ley	Slaggy-ford	Alston		
	s d	s d	s d	s d	s d	s d		p.m.
NEWCASTLE dep. 9 40 a.m.	7/6	8/0	8/0	8/0	9/0	9/6	Alston .. .. dep.	7 50
Hexham ,, 10 11	3/6	4/6	4/6	4/9	5/6	6/0	Slaggyford .. .. ,,	8 0
							Lambley .. .. ,,	8 15
							Coanwood .. .. ,,	8 20
							Featherstone Park ,,	8 30
							Haltwhistle .. .. ,,	8 30
	a.m.	a.m.	a.m.	a.m.	a.m.	a.m.	Hexham .. .. ,,	8 55
Arrival Times	10 40	10 50	10 55	11 0	11 10	11 22	NEWCASTLE arr.	9 30

Children under three years of age, free; three years and under 14 years, half-fares
(fractions of 1d. charged as 1d.)

CHARGES FOR BICYCLES ACCOMPANYING PASSENGERS WILL BE AT THE SPECIAL
RATE OF HALF THE ABOVE PASSENGER FARES FOR THE RETURN JOURNEY.
(Fractions of 1d. charged as 1d.)

TICKETS CAN BE OBTAINED IN ADVANCE
FROM THE STATIONS AND ACCREDITED RAIL TICKET AGENCIES

Further information will be supplied on application to the stations, agencies, or to K. N.
Sidebotham, District Passenger Supt., British Railways, Newcastle, Tel. 2-0741.

Published by British Railways   (N.E. Region)   3/61   Printed in Great Britain   Ellesmere, Skipton— C3½

A railway excursion on the Alston branch, 1961

Public utilities

The 1920's saw Alston Rural District Council's commitment to local authority housing. At first, three blocks of four 'Parlour Cottages' were proposed to be built in Alston next to the workhouse, now Fairhill Cottages, near the cemetery, and plans were drawn but the scheme came to nothing. Instead two pairs of substantial semi-detached houses were built on Nenthead Road and Jollybeard Lane. The Firs housing estate was started in the 1940's, at the same time that a town centre bypass was proposed from the Tyne Bridge alongside the cemetery to the Primary School gates and across the Fairhill to join the Nenthead Road. In the 1950's a large area of Alston town centre was demolished. The car park between the Co-op and the Post Office is the site of a collection of houses, pubs, offices and shops. Houses opposite the church gates and houses at the bottom of Kates Lane were also demolished to allow Church Road to be opened up for housing and for Grisedale Croft to be built. In the 1960's Hillhouse Lane and Park View Lane were built. Meanwhile, council houses were built at Leadgate, in Garrigill, alongside the village green and towards Gatehead, and at Bevin Terrace and Vicarage Terrace in Nenthead.

In 1948/49, 99% of people within the water supply area were supplied with mains water from springs at a rate of 39 gallons per head per day, but buildings between Nenthead and Alston were without a piped supply.

In the early years of the century sewage disposal was still very basic. Dr. Stuart Carson gave his report as Medical Officer to the R.D.C meeting of March 1901 and recommended that there should be *"Public Ashpits for all three main communities, with a month's trial of house to house collection"*. It was ordered that a six month trial would be given. Dr. Carson reported to the same meeting that the death rate was exceeding the birth rate. During the previous quarter there had been 3.19 deaths per thousand, and 2.23 births per thousand. He had condemned four cottages in the Butts as unfit for habitation, and investigated the purity of the water supply at the high end of Garrigill. Diahorrea had been prevalent in the area, and the school at Nenthall had been closed from 4th June to 13th July due to whooping cough.

Alston continued to be heated and lit with gas from the Alston Gas Co. Ltd. In the period between 1938 and 1948, Alston saw one of the four greatest percentage increases in gas production in the county, almost doubling its output.

In 1949, the company was nationalised, becoming part of the Hexham Division of the Northern Gas Board, which, in 1951, had a larger storage tank installed in Alston, built by a firm from Stockton. 1956 saw the closure of Hexham works when it became part of a grid main, but Alston was too remote for inclusion. Here, coal-gas and coke production continued until 1960, when a butane/air plant was installed, the first in the Cumberland Division area, going into operation in June, with gas delivered by road tankers. This development meant the closure of the solid fuel retorts and all customers' appliances had to be converted.

The winter of 1962/63, gave the Gas Board some anxiety due to snow-blocked roads, but in the event there was never any need to restrict supply to customers. However, as a safeguard for supply against severe conditions in the future, an additional storage tank had to be installed. In 1964 a 7,000 cu.ft. gas holder arrived from the recently-closed gasworks at Seascale, which for transportation had first to be cut into four pieces then welded together again on site in Alston. This was the holder's third home, having originally been used in an engineering works at Stockton.

Due mainly to the high price of Butane/LPG (liquid petroleum gas) the Gas Board had supplied gas at a financial loss to Alston and towns like it. However with the availability of North Sea gas, (which Alston had missed out on in the 1960's) combined with technological advances, it became possible to pipe natural gas through polyethylene mains and viable for Alston to be incorporated into the National Grid, supplying 2 to 2½ million cu.ft. per year. So, in 1987, the old railway trackbed from Haltwhistle was used for another purpose - that of providing a route for the new gas supply pipe, and the old works were finally closed and dismantled, 144 years after the first lighting up.

Mains electricity had arrived on Alston Moor in 1934 and was described as being 'available' in the 1938 trades directory, but Nenthead's streets had been lit by electricity long before that.

On 2nd January 1920 members of the Nenthead Ward met to consider, *"the adoption of the Lighting and Watching Act 1833 and any other business arising therefrom"*. The Chairman, Councillor R.C. Bell, gave particulars of the Act and how the cost was to be met. After some discussion a committee was appointed, *"to inquire into the cost of lighting the village either by Oil Lamps, Gas or Electricity"*. After this the meeting was adjourned.

The new committee approached the Vieille Montagne Zinc Company to ask if they would *"be inclined"* to grant a connection from their internal electric lighting system to at least three points in the village. The Company replied that they would indeed be willing and the three points chosen were The Stone Bridge, The Rails (to Overwater), and Nenthead Street.

The Company's terms were that: The Company was to provide and erect the lamps at its own cost. The Company was not to be held responsible for any interruption in the lighting provision. They reserved the right to withdraw the lights at any time. That any light wilfully damaged would not be replaced. The charge to be paid to the Company was 1 shilling (5p) per lamp per year.

At the March Ward Meeting acceptance of this offer was, understandably, carried unanimously. In view of this the Ward Committee decided not to adopt the Lighting and Watching Act of 1833. The Chairman and Secretary were appointed to collect the nominal three shillings per year for the lights and Rev. W. Taylor proposed that, *"notices be painted on the lamp standards warning persons against doing wilful damage to the installation"*.

At the Annual Meeting of 1920 the princely sum of 3s.8d. was collected. 3s. went to the V.M. and the extra 8d was retained for postages.

The cottage hospital

As early as 1895, the Rural District Council had discussed the suggestion that Alston Moor should have its own trained nurse as well as a G.P., but it had no powers to act. In 1902 the council searched unsuccessfully for a site for an isolation hospital and suggested that Haltwhistle Council should be approached to join in the venture. Then in July 1906 plans for a new hospital were approved.

Parade float in aid of the proposed hospital

The Ruth Lancaster James Cottage Hospital was opened on 23rd July 1908, after a donation of £5,000 by that lady. She was said to have been prompted to do this by her concern about the numbers of mining accidents which occurred so far from a hospital. The hospital opened with nine beds, two cots, accommodation for the nurses and the three acre field in front of the hospital that was bought to ensure enjoyable views for the patients and staff in perpetuity. The hospital has been extended several times since opening. The first time was in 1929 when a new wing was opened as a memorial to the long-practising doctor of Alston Moor, Dr. Stewart Carson. He had succeeded his father in practice and had been the Moor's G.P. for forty-five years. In 1945, two more wards and a surgery were added. The hospital was extended again in 1950, when an operating theatre was built, capable of catering for general surgery, and at the same time facilities were installed for physiotherapy. A day centre was built, known as 'The Bungalow' for the elderly, and another expansion took place in 1994, when an extension to house the clinic was opened. In 1998, the clinic was extended yet again. After threats of closure in the first decade of the twenty-first century Alston, in common with many other small towns, is hanging on to its precious cottage hospital

The first nurses at the new hospital

Religion

As with everywhere else in the country, church and chapel attendance on Alston Moor has declined. The Quaker meetings ceased in 1902; this small sect had met since the early seventeen hundreds. However, the Meeting House in Alston has been renovated and reopened and a small group again meets regularly.

Even the Methodist congregation declined to the point when the two branches amalgamated in 1932. Eventually all the outlying Methodist chapels at Nenthead, Nentsbury, Nest, Brownside (Leadgate), and Garrigill closed, as well as the two Congregationalist chapels at Redwing and Alston. The chapel buildings are usually deconsecrated then sold for conversion to houses.

A Sunday School demonstration, 1914

St. Paul's Methodist Church at Townhead in Alston was the last to close and Alston Methodists now hold services in the Catholic Church of St. Wulstan in Kings Arms Lane, which is a relatively recent addition to the area, and gives a good example of religious co-operation. The Church of England churches at Alston, Garrigill and Nenthead remain open with the vicars forming part of a team circuit with the rest of South Tynedale.

Wesleyan Chapel, Garrigill

Education

The Balfour Education Act of 1902 was followed by the opening of the
Samuel King's County Council Secondary School in Alston in 1909, which

is now the Primary School. The school was so called because of the educational charity bequeathed by Glasgow businessman Samuel King, in memory of his mother's birthplace.

The opening of the new school led to the closure of the old Grammar School, which later became one of the country's smallest fire stations and a change of status for the 'High' School, from an Elementary to a mixed Primary School. The Salvin Schools in the Butts combined to become the Infants' School.

The new Secondary School had accommodation for eighty children, taught by six teachers, with free places for children who passed the scholarship exam, and in 1910 the average attendance was fifty. A 1925 guidebook describes staff at Samuel King's School as, "highly qualified university graduates". Fees in that year were £10.15s. per annum, inclusive of books, but in 1929 the school governors voted to reduce the fees to £6 because of the general hardship in the area. In 1948, thirteen pupils from the High School passed the scholarship exam, together with five from Nenthead, two from Nenthall, and one from Garrigill.

Another reorganisation occurred in 1957 when the present Samuel King's School opened, with a roll of about 180, having been built at a cost of £92,500. In the new school, 'Grammar' and 'Modern' streams were combined. This led to the closure of the High School, as pupils were transferred from there and from the old Samuel King's to the new school. Part of the press report of 17th September 1957 read:

"Centrally situated on a steeply sloping site to the West of Church Road, the school has a magnificent outlook over the Alston fells. Maximum use has been made of colour in order to provide a stimulating and lively environment for the children".

The opening of the new Samuel King's School was also followed by the closure of the Infants' Schools in the Butts, when pupils moved up to the old Samuel King's School that became the Primary School. The work to convert the building had been carried out by Kearton's, the local builders, and cost £11,250. The school had places for 150 pupils and it officially opened in March 1960.

The first Samuel King's School under construction

In the outlying village schools attendances had dwindled as people left the area, until the schools were no longer viable. In the first year of the century, Tynehead had eight pupils, but despite this low number it lasted until 1933. Leadgate in 1901 had about twenty pupils and closed in the 1932. Nenthall clung on to its school until about 1950, then after closure it was demolished and the stone was used in alterations to Alston Foundry. Garrigill school had about seventy-five children on its register in 1901 and it remained open until the reorganisation of the 1950's when, after centuries of education in the village, it too closed.

The primary school at Nenthead was built as a 'Board' school in 1899 to replace the one built by the London Lead Company in 1864 that is now the village hall. In 2010 the school is still very much alive and well, with about thirty children on its register, a marked decrease from 1901 when average attendance was 140.

Fairs

The fairs of previous centuries began to change with the times. A newspaper of June 1918 reported;

> *"Tradition tells us that Alston was, once upon a time, a much busier place than it is today. It was a market town in the true sense. Every Saturday the two market squares (the present Market Place and the Potato Market outside the Post Office) were filled with all kinds of produce brought in carts from far and near, and a busy throng met to do business in the old fashioned way. At regular intervals in the spring and autumn the fairs were held, and one of the greatest days of the year was that of May Fair, when cattle and sheep filled the Fairhill. A horse fair of no mean importance was held on the Garrigill road, and every available space on each side of the street at the Townhead would be packed with carts laden with young pigs. The market carts filled the market squares, while there were all sorts of stalls and shows catering to the fantastic tastes of a motley throng that surged upon the street. 'In them days yan could walk on heeds o' people frae Toonheed to Toonfoot.'*
>
> *Thursday of last week was May Fair Day. The early hours of a glorious May day saw the dusty highways occupied by a continuous stream of traffic. All roads led to Alston, and people came in traps, on horseback and on cycles over every hill and through every vale, and crowds poured into the old town By eleven o'clock, one could scarcely go up or down the street without being accosted by a perspiring farmer leading a horse, asking where there was likely to be any stable room. It was, however, the first time that the May Fair was not held. Having held its place when nearly all the other fairs have ceased to be, it was this time completely ousted by the new market established by the Alston Moor Auction Mart, Ltd., who arranged a 'Great Special Sale' (of livestock) on the occasion."*

The opinion of the publication was that, *"when the war is over, the May Day Special will become something like a gala day"*.

Two prize winning sheep

Trade, industry and employment

The two remaining corn mills in the 20th century were both in Alston. The High Mill (Lancaster's) closed in the 1930's, and Low Mill (Haldon's) closed in the 1950's and was demolished. The saw mill, which had also supplied marble and granite memorials as a 'speciality', closed in the 1920's when its owner, Herbert Richardson retired.

At the old Brewery, the Alston Hosiery Works took over from George Storey and later the buildings became a laundry owned by Miss Blackett-Ord of Brownside near Leadgate. Later still a clothing factory was established there.

Employment prospects were bleak in 1987 when Alston Moor had the highest unemployment rate in the county at 24%. The percentage of unemployed dropped to 10.3% in 1991, only to rise again to 13.0% in 1994, then falling to 10.5% in 1995. There was further gloom when the firm of Kearton's, who were local builders of some renown and employed fifty-eight workers in 1991, went into liquidation in 1994. Kearton's had been an Alston family business in existence for four generations.

Attempts to attract industry to this area, as with many other areas, included construction of 'Advance Factories' in the 1970's at the old Station Yard in Alston, and at Nenthead, and later industrial units at Skelgillside on the Nenthead Road out of the town were built in Alston in the 1990's. The Advance Factory at the Station Yard was in industrial use only for a short time, the rest of its time was spent empty until rented by the South Tyne Railway as a carriage shed, and the Skellgillside units took a long time to be fully occupied. After many years in business the Advance Factory at Nenthead is empty.

Precision Products, started in 1947 by Roger Ball, who took over the patent Shaw casting process, is very successfully making and selling high quality stainless steel and super-alloy castings. The firm is now the largest employer on Alston Moor, and it is still expanding under new ownership as 'Bond's Precision Products'.

Population

For eighty or so years of the 20th century, people continued to leave Alston Moor. In a survey of 1948, the Alston with Garrigill district was the only local authority in Cumberland where the population of 1948 was less than that of 1939, and the population post war was continuing to decrease. Then, as now, remoteness of the area did not lend itself to industrial or economic development; there was no incentive for manufacturers to move here and there were no local resources to develop.

Between 1921 and 1948, the population of Alston-with-Garrigill dropped from 3,344 to 2,190, a massive fall of 34.5%. The nearest rival in the county was Millom with a fall of 17.4%. Carlisle, by contrast, had gained 21.2%. However, between 1948 and 1950, the numbers actually increased from 2,190 to over 2,300, reaching the latter figure for the first time since 1939. But this itself was a peak, for in 1961 the census showed a decrease to 2,105, and again in 1971 down to the all-time low of 1,916. The population for 1981 showed a slight increase to 1,932, and it increased again to 2,065 in 1991. The population seems to have stabilised around this figure as the mid-year estimate for 2008 was 2,085, however this is still less than it was thirty years before.

Recreation

The fifteen pubs of Alston in 1901 dwindled to five, a sharp decrease from the twenty-three of 1847. Names such as the Royal Oak, the Ewe & Lamb, the King's Arms, the Weary Sportsman, Shaw House on the Hartside road, the Golden Lion, and, more recently the Crown and the Blue Bell, have all disappeared. The Hare and Hounds at Nenthall and the Horse and Waggon at Nentsberry have gone. Nenthead's three pubs have decreased to one, the Miners' Arms. The George and Dragon at Garrigill closed recently, while a house name in the village still records the 'Fox Inn'.

As an alternative to alcohol there used to be the lemonade factory opposite what is now the Primary School. This was in the days when pop bottles had glass 'marble' stoppers put in by machine. A former resident of Alston remembered that as a little girl;

> *"We stood and watched the bottles going round very quick so the fizz in the bottles forced the glass marble up into the neck of the bottle, which was quite hard to push down when you wanted a drink. The lemonade man was called Mr. Pratt and he took the lemonade round the shops with a horse and flat cart and a Labrador which travelled with him."*

Nenthead cricket team

Alston Brass ensemble' at Templecroft, c.1905

Opening of Golf Course
Easter monday 1906

The opening of Alston's first golf course, Easter Monday 1906

Between the wars, as well as Alston Moor's own decline, came the economic depression of the 1930's. This was countered in part by various public works schemes, notably the filling in and landscaping of the Fairhill Recreation Ground, which had been bought for the people of Alston from the Admiralty in 1899. This led to the creation of a tennis court, a football pitch of sorts, and a bowling green; but the proposed swimming pool, a facility which would be appreciated today, was never built. Garrigill and Nenthead both have their well-equipped playgrounds and open space for recreation and an allotment association has recently been established in Garrigill. For a time Alston had its own cinema, in operation from the 1930's to the 1950's, with its corrugated iron roof giving extra sound effects on rainy nights. A nine-hole golf course was constructed some distance from Alston on the Penrith road in 1906 which moved to a site on the Hexham road in 1924, before moving to its present site on the Middleton road. It must have provided a challenge to find a suitable piece of land but the views from the course rate among the best in the country. During severe winters the ski slope on the Middleton Road is very popular. On one occasion during the winter of 2009/2010, the author counted approximately eighty cars parked by the roadside there. The Coast-to-Coast cycle route keeps Alston Moor on the tourist map, as does the Pennine Way long distance walk. Otherwise, Alston Moor is the place for a quiet holiday and a convenient base for exploring other areas.

PERSONALITIES OF ALSTON MOOR

Westgarth Forster

Westgarth Forster was a celebrated mineralogist and mining expert. In 1908, according to Caesar Caine, his name was still a household word in Garrigill and the surrounding district, as well as in other mining centres. His work entitled 'A Treatise on the strata from Newcastle-upon-Tyne to Cross Fell with remarks on Mineral Veins, etc', can still be regarded as a work of reference. The following biography is edited from the introduction to the third edition of his book, edited by Rev. William Nall.

Westgarth Forster was born in 1772 and was the eldest of eight children. His father, also named Westgarth, occupied the post of Manager of the Allendale Mines, and upon his death in 1797, Westgarth junior was appointed his successor. He held this post until 1807, when he resigned and moved in with his sister Susan who occupied the family home and farm at Ivy House in Garrigill. After this time he alternated the duties of a farmer with researches for his book which appeared in 1809. Its publication laid the foundations for English geology.

In 1810 he became a mine surveyor, and continued in this profession until 1833. A second edition of his 'Strata' appeared in 1821. During this period his energies led him far beyond the mineral areas of the North. He worked in Wales, in distant English counties such as Somerset, and also in the mining regions of Spain and North America. He met with a measure of financial success, and in his most prosperous days his income ran easily into four figures. But reverses set in, and in the closing years of life he was saddened by successive financial losses, caused by what has been called a mania for mining speculations.

At the 'winning of the hay' in 1833 he walked into Garrigill practically a penniless man. The following year he parted with his plate, pictures, and books, in order to obtain daily sustenance, and he died at Ivy House, as recorded on his tombstone, November 9th, 1835.

Caesar Caine has the last word when he says, *"Repeated misfortune had undermined his health, and he died poor and depressed in spirit."*

Ruth Lancaster James

Ruth was born Ruth Lancaster Dickinson, the daughter of Joseph and Ruth Dickinson. Her father was the third son of John and Mary Dickinson of Low Byer, her grandfather John Dickinson and her uncle Thomas, Joseph's oldest brother, were in turn Moormasters for the Greenwich Hospital, the Lords of the Manor of Alston Moor.

John Dickinson moved from Annat Walls near Alston in about 1789 with his wife Mary and their first batch of four children to Low Byer, where they proceeded to have another five, including Joseph. Joseph married Ruth Rowell in the Non Conformist chapel, on the 28th October 1823. Next year their daughter was baptised Ruth Lancaster Dickinson on the 26th August 1824, however Ruth was to be their only child.

For a time Joseph was a Spirit Merchant in Alston, then the trades directory of 1829 shows two entries for him, one as 'Joseph Dickinson & Co., Tallow Chandlers', the other as 'Joseph Dickinson, Land Surveyor'. Joseph's oldest brother, Thomas, had returned to Alston from Grassington in Yorkshire, where he had been a mine agent, to succeed their father as Moor Master and to join Joseph in the lucrative sideline of tallow chandlers, making candles to sell to the lead miners. By 1834 the trades directory description of their business was 'Joseph and Thomas Dickinson & Co., Tallow Chandlers', and by this time the brothers were included with the 'Gentry and Clergy' of Alston.

Family life was tragically short for Ruth, she was only seven years old when her mother died at the age of thirty-nine on 21st July 1831. Joseph did not marry again and the first detailed national census in 1841 shows him living on his own at Townfoot in Alston with one female servant. By then Ruth was sixteen and she was not at home. The 1841 census showed the only Ruth Dickinson in England to be a Ruth Dickinson, aged sixteen, who may or may not be ours, and Anne Dickinson, aged eighteen, both of independent means, staying as guests of a family at Middlethorpe near Londesborough in Yorkshire.

The following year a Ruth Dickinson, aged twenty, sailed from Liverpool on board the ship the 'Thomas P. Cope' to arrive in Philadelphia on 25th August 1842. Was this our Ruth, with an inaccurately recorded age? She would have the wealth, independence and the education to travel, which was normal for one of her background.

In 1851 Joseph was still a land surveyor living at Townfoot. Where Ruth was we don't know, at twenty-six she might have been anywhere. She might have been living in Alston two years later, when her father Joseph died in 1853 at the age of fifty-eight and was buried on the 16th September. Certainly in the census of 1861 she was living in 'Main Street', Alston, as the head of the household, consisting of herself and one female servant. At thirty-six years of age and unmarried she described herself as a 'Landed Proprietor'. Then in the directory of 1869 'Miss Ruth L. Dickinson' was listed in the 'Gentry and Clergy' of Alston.

Ruth must have travelled, for she was able to meet Daniel James, a widower twenty-two years her senior, who had been born in New York but had become a naturalised British subject. He arrived in England sometime between 1830 and 1832 and lived as a merchant in the metal trade at Beaconsfield, Little Woolton in Lancashire. In 1871, when Daniel was sixty-eight, Ruth, who by then was forty-six, was staying as his guest with her friend Lucy Arrow from Kent and her daughter, also called Lucy Arrow, with Daniel and three of his sons at their home. Daniel must have been a very successful merchant since he was able to send his sons, who were in their late teens, to Cambridge University and to employ five female servants, a gardener, two under-gardeners and a coachman.

Romance must have already been in the air and perhaps Lucy Arrow and her daughter were at Beaconsfield as chaperones, for Ruth became Daniel James's third wife and stepmother to his seven grown-up children when she married him at St. Augustine's Church in Alston on 5th July 1871. In the church register, Daniel was described as being of full age, a widower, and a merchant of Beaconsfield, Liverpool, the son of Nathaniel E. James. Ruth was of full age, a spinster of Alston, the daughter of Joseph Dickinson.

It would seem that the couple travelled to the United States on at least one occasion. In 1874 Daniel James, nationality English, a merchant aged seventy and his wife, recorded on the passenger list as 'Rachel', departed on the ship 'Cuba' from Liverpool and arrived in New York on 23rd October.

Sadly, Ruth and Daniel did not have long together, for on the 27th November 1876, Daniel died. Ruth continued to live at Beaconsfield with a retinue of five female servants and a gardener for the rest of her life. The ten-yearly census returns describe her as an annuitant living off her own means.

Mrs. James took an active and caring interest in her birthplace. After the Fairhill Recreation Ground was established on the last day of 1899, she paid off the debts of the Trustees, then, in looking for another local cause, it was suggested that she might support the initiative for a Cottage Hospital. In 1907 she gave an endowment of £5,000 to the Cottage Hospital Fund. Unfortunately Ruth did not live to see the opening of the hospital in July 1908, for she died on 4th April 1907, aged eighty-two. In her honour the hospital was named the Ruth Lancaster James Cottage Hospital.

Wilhelmina Martha James, O.B.E.
(the author Austin Clare)

Wilhelmina Martha James was born on 3rd May 1846, the oldest of six sisters and three brothers born to Rev. Octavius James, a rather eccentric vicar who lived at Clarghyll Hall. Octavius was the vicar and architect of the church at Kirkhaugh. For many years he was on the Alston Moor Board of Guardians and he was also a noted cattle breeder.

In the main, Wilhelmina, known as Patty, led the quiet life of a Victorian spinster. She took the Sunday School at her father's church, where she attended dutifully each Sunday. With her mother and sisters she went to tea and received friends to tea. She went with her mother to London for a month or two each year; they later changed the venue to Torquay. However, she was a prolific authoress, who probably took the man's pseudonym of Austin Clare to gain credibility as a writer, and she may have been an admirer of Jane Austen. Most of her books which were published by the Society for the Promotion of Christian Knowledge.

She sometimes wrote in a strong local dialect, which could account for her not having attained lasting fame. Another reason could be that she was one of the school of authors who revelled in moralistic tales with such titles as, 'The Siege Perilous; How I Learnt To Sit In It; Being The History Of His Selfish Youth', published in 1898. Other titles include 'Randal of Randleholm' (a work with a local theme), 'The Carved Cartoon', 'The Conscience of Dr. Holt', 'A Child of Menhir', 'A Pearl in the Shell', 'By the Rise of the River', 'Pandora's Portion: A Story of Hope' and 'Another Man's Burden'.

Clarghyll Hall

Then at the age of sixty-nine, together with her sister Mabel, Wilhelmina served with the British Red Cross during the First World War. In August 1915 she travelled to Salonika in Greece to work with the Serbians at Monastir near the Greek border. She was the senior Red Cross worker there and earned official recognition when she was mentioned in army despatches in March 1917. For her services she was awarded the Royal Serbian Order of St. Sava, Fifth Class by Crown Prince Alexander of Serbia. The letter of notification from Lt. Col. H. Fitzpatrick on 1st May 1918, read, *"we have always been proud of your fine record of self sacrificing work, for which I hope you will soon receive due recognition"*. Soon afterwards she was awarded the O.B.E.

In the late 1920's, when she was over eighty years old, she sailed to Canada to visit her brother Hugh and other relatives. On her return to

England she lived in a private hotel on the south coast and continued her charitable work for the Red Cross. Even though Wilhelmina was in poor health, she read to the blind until the day before her death in 1932. She was cremated and her ashes scattered outside the door of Kirkhaugh church.

John Little and Cross Fell Mine

Anyone who has read about the lead mines of the north Pennines will be aware of the phenomenal success of the Hudgill Burn mine, which, over a relatively short time from 1814, produced vast quantities of lead and silver to make huge profits for the partnership of leaseholder/miners. From the scant records available, it would appear that there was a predecessor to the Hudgill phenomenon. The Crossfell Vein was discovered in 1805 and worked with great success by John Little of Raise House in Alston.

John Little was born in 1773, the fourth child of Edward and Sarah Little. Edward was a farmer who lived at several places in succession around Alston Moor before finally coming to rest at Flatt, half way between Alston and Garrigill.

John married Sarah Walton in 1795, in 1800 he was described as a farmer but by 1803 he was a lead mine agent. He was a mine agent at the beginning of 1805 when he discovered the Cross Fell lead vein. The event was described as follows; *"Little, on his return from Appleby Fair, his horse having, in coming down an Old Brooken Way, removed a portion from the Surface of the vein, and exposed some ore to the view , which being observed by Mr. Little, who lost no time in Securing a Lease of Sir Michael Flemming of Prydall Hall near Ambleside, formed a Company and commenced mining operations immediately which were Attended with great Success".*

The vein was very rich near the surface and for a fairly short time Cross Fell was the most productive mine yielding nearly 5,000 bings of lead ore (2,000 tons) per annum when the average price per bing was £5.10s. The quantity of ore being raised made it worthwhile for John Little to invest in building his own smelt mill on Cross Fell to smelt the lead ore.

With his new-found wealth John quickly moved up in the world to live at Raise House at Alston where, in 1807, he described his status as a "yeoman".

Part of the account of the discovery of Cross fell vein by John Little

The wealth produced by the Crossfell Mine also brought out the philanthropic side of John Little's character and he is credited with spending much of his fortune for the benefit of the town of Alston. Mackenzie MacBride in his booklet 'Quaint Alston', published in 1923, claims that John Little, as the largest proprietor of Cross Fell mine, paved the streets of Alston, gave oil lamps for the streets, was instrumental in bringing water to the town and brought the town its first printing press. Unfortunately nothing more is known about these enterprises, except that, on the list of benefactors for the water supply in about 1808, he is second only to the Greenwich Hospital, the Lords of the Manor.

Sadly, John Little did not live very long to enjoy his wealth and acclaim, he died at Raise House on 6th June 1821 at the age of forty-seven. In 1833 Thomas Sopwith wrote a good deal about Hudgill mine in his book, but made no mention of Crossfell Mine. This could be an indication that it was finished by then and its memory had been overshadowed by the impact of Hudgill.

Hugh Lee Pattinson

Hugh Lee Pattinson, F.R.S., F.R.A.S., F.G.S.

Hugh was a man of many parts, chemist, astronomer, metallurgist, scientist and photographer. The trades directory entry for Alston, 1901, gave the following biography;

"Hugh Lee Pattinson, whose fame has extended far beyond the limits of this kingdom, was born here (in Alston) on Christmas Day 1796. His father (Thomas), a member of the Society of Friends, kept a shop in the town.

Hugh received such an education as was obtainable in those days at a good country school. His strong reasoning and inventive powers he displayed in early youth, and whilst still a boy he astonished his friends and companions by the construction of an electrical machine and the wonderful effects he produced. He was ever eager in the pursuit of knowledge, and with such apparatus only as he could make himself, he acquired the rudiments of chemistry and one or two experimental sciences. He was at this time, Dr. Lonsdale tell us in the Worthies of Cumberland, 'like a bit of good ore imbedded in a gangue or matrix - the stony surroundings had to be washed from the more precious metal, and the metal itself ground and polished to its proper uses.'

Tired of his circumscribed field of action and the absence of facilities for prosecuting his favourite sciences, (in 1821) he went to Newcastle, where he obtained the situation of clerk and assistant to a soap boiler. In 1822 he joined the Literary and Philosophical Society of Newcastle. In 1825, the office of assayist for the lead mines of Alston became vacant; he applied and received the appointment. Whilst assay-master to the Commissioners, he first appeared before the world as an author. He contributed two papers to the 'Philosophical Magazine'; one was entitled 'The action of steam and quicklime upon heated galena', and the other 'The fossil trees found in Jefferies Rake Vein at Derwent Lead Mine, in the County of Durham'. In 1831 he published an admirable description of the ore hearth and the mode of constructing it.

Pattinson was at this time directing the whole power of his penetrating intellect to the discovery of some more perfect and economical method of extracting the silver from the lead than the one then in use. His efforts were at length crowned with success in 1829. By the Pattinson method the extraction of silver from lead could be profitably pursued down to a minimum of 3oz to the ton; previous to this time the extraction of the precious metal was not remunerative when the proportion was less than 20oz to the ton. His discovery brought him £16,000, he was appointed manager of the Beaumont lead works in 1831 and in 1834 entered into partnership with two other gentlemen, and established the now famous chemical works at Felling, near Gateshead.

Here he discovered a ready and inexpensive process for the manufacture of carbonate of magnesia, which has displaced all other makes in the market.

Mr. Pattinson devoted much of his time to the study of astronomy and the physical sciences, and was highly esteemed no less for his urbanity than for the extent of his knowledge, by the most eminent scientists of the day. He was elected a Fellow of the Royal Society, and also of the Astronomical and Geological Societies of London. He was also Vice President of the British Association from 1838 to 1852.

He retired to study astronomy, mathematics and physics. He died in 1858 at his home at Scot's House near Gateshead and was interred at Washington, in the county of Durham."

There is only a little more information to add. As a chemist Hugh Pattinson was interested in the development of photography and when he visited Canada in 1840 he took some very early daguerreotype images of Niagara Falls. It is possible that Pattinson himself appears on one of the photo's since they took about fifteen or thirty minutes for exposure, he would have ample time to put himself into the frame.

In addition to the establishment of the Felling Chemical Works in 1833, Hugh Pattinson then set up a factory in Washington in 1842 for the production of white lead and then magnesia for pharmaceutical use. Hugh's son left the firm in 1849 to rejoin the Felling Chemical Works. After Hugh's death all four of his sons-in-law continued the white lead business.

During his later life, Hugh Lee Pattinson did not lose contact with his native town; the year before he died he laid the foundation stone to Alston's Town Hall.

Rt. Hon. Sir William Stephenson, Bart.

Unfortunately, we know precious little about William Stephenson, Lord Mayor of London. He was the son of Henry Stephenson of Crosslands near Alston, the lessee of the coal mine at the head of Gilderdale on Alston Moor. In 1723 Gilderdale colliery was the only coal mine worth the Lord's Rent, for in that year on 11th July, in a "Rental of Estate of the Earl of Derwentwater" for "A Colliery att Hartside ffell", Henry Stephenson was due to pay two instalments of rent per year at Martinmas and Whitsuntide of £5.2s.6d., in total £10.5s.0d.

When Henry died he was buried in a privileged place inside St.

Augustine's Church on 30th April 1734 and the coal mine was taken over by his son, John.

The Market Cross, as illustrated in one of Austin Clare's books

We know something of John, who retained a local connection. John Stephenson became Sheriff of Newcastle in 1728 then in 1730 he bought Knarsdale Hall for £2,600 from the Wallis family who had fallen on hard times. In 1747 when John became an alderman of Newcastle, he was also the owner of Hunwich and Rogerly in County Durham, and he had interest in Coxlodge Colliery near Newcastle.

John died in 1761 and by his will, made in 1759, he established what became known as 'Stephenson's Charity' of Alston and Garrigill, by which £4 a year was given to sixteen poor widows of the parish. The Charity also applied to Knarsdale and Kirkhaugh where 5/- each was given to eight poor widows in both parishes and if there were not enough women then the difference was made up with poor men. The money was distributed by the minister and churchwardens each Christmas Day.

The little we know about William is that he was possibly born at Crosslands near Alston, he went to London, whether to seek his fortune or whether he already had one we can't say, but he probably arrived as a man of substance. In 1754 he was elected Alderman of Bridge Ward Within. He became Sheriff in 1757 and he was elected Lord Mayor of London in 1764. What he had done to deserve this honour is not known but to be mayor was an expensive business, because the banquets, parades, favours, gifts, etc., all had to be paid for personally by the mayor.

Nevertheless, in celebration, William gave money for the erection of a Market Cross in his home town of Alston on land given by the Greenwich Hospital, the Lords of the Manor. The cross took the form of a covered market, similar to the present one, which was opened in 1766. William also contributed towards the rebuilding of St. Augustine's Church in 1769. In 1773 he was once more an alderman of London just before his death in 1774.

Jacob Walton

The only memorial outside of a church or churchyard on Alston Moor, apart from two war memorials and the Market Cross, is uniquely a memorial to a lead mine owner and 'adventurer', Jacob Walton.

Jacob Walton was born in 1809 into a family of lead mining adventurers. He had eight brothers, most of whom became lead mining agents, but Jacob soon became the most prominent.

At his peak, Jacob Walton ran one of the two most successful independent mining companies, he was equal second to the London Lead Company as lessees from the Greenwich Hospital, the other company was owned by the Attwood Brothers. Jacob Walton employed hundreds of men, owned many lead mines and, with his brothers, owned four smelt mills. He not only mined lead, he held the leases and explored for coal, copper, zinc, witherite, and iron stone. He operated on Alston Moor, in Weardale and Teesdale and further, to the south west of Scotland and to the west of Cumbria. He was described as having opened up many mines, and as being instrumental in bringing the railway to Alston.

Jacob Walton had a great enthusiasm for work and a great talent to spot a good lead vein. As a result he was continually asked for advice by other companies and his presence on the list of shareholders of any mine was a mark of credibility. As early as the 1840's Jacob claimed he had more to do with the Greenwich Hospital agents than any man in the region and every time they placed unlimited confidence in him. This consultancy was, on one occasion, requested at a national level when an impartial adviser was needed for a government commission. This was in addition to managing his own mines, and there were eventually about twenty-four of those.

Jacob Walton lived most of his life at Greenends near Nenthead. By his wife Phoebe he was father to five daughters and two sons. He was what we now call a workaholic and it is probable that his many activities led to a decline in his health. In the autumn of 1861, he suffered an illness from which he did not make a full recovery. Jacob made his will in September 1862 and died in March 1863. The Carlisle Journal described him as one of the ablest and most successful mine owners in the north and reported that, *"The deceased was an extensive mining proprietor of considerable ability, and will be deeply regretted, both by the working classes and by all who knew him. His remains were interred at Alston Cemetery on 6th March, when, as a mark of respect, the shops were all closed"*.

The workmen who were employed at Jacob's Fallowfield Mine near Hexham thought so highly of him that after his death they started a collection for some personal testimonial to his memory, but when the scheme became known to the public, the public asked to be allowed to take part and they also contributed to a memorial to him.

The Walton Memorial was built in Alston the next year, about where the road signs at Townfoot are now. The inauguration ceremony took place on the 18th November 1864 and in spite of the miserable weather a large number of residents of Alston Moor and the surrounding districts gathered in Alston Market Square. The crowd included about 120 workmen employed at Fallowfield, who had travelled up the Tyne valley. At one o'clock the crowd was arranged in rows four deep and they marched in procession to Townfoot where the unveiling ceremony was held.

The memorial stood for almost a hundred years until 1960 when it was removed by the County Council to make way for a road-widening scheme. At the time the Cumberland and Westmorland Herald wondered *"whether the whole of this displaced monument should be replaced, or just the portion bearing the inscription, will be a matter for the authorities concerned to decide, but certainly there ought to be some permanent reminder of a man who, in his day, was considered so deserving of honour"*.

The inscribed plaque was inserted into a wall nearby but the rest of the monument lay in pieces in a local quarry for forty-four years, then with funding from the National Lottery it was rebuilt and on Tuesday 6th July 2004, unveiled once more.

John and Jacob Wilson and Hudgill Mine

The story of the discovery and subsequent great wealth of the Hudgill Burn lead mine is the stuff of legend.

During the early years of the nineteenth century the Flow Edge Mining Company had spent £2000 in an exploratory trial to discover a rich lead vein under Middle Fell before giving up in 1808. Then in 1812 the brothers John and Jacob Wilson and their partners applied to continue the trial. The events were recounted by Thomas Sopwith in 1833 when he wrote,

"In 1812, John and Jacob Wilson, with some other experienced miners, obtained leave to pursue the trial, and accordingly having arched the entrance to the level, cleared out the old workings, and laid new rails, they continued the main level of the former company, but altered its direction a little to the south".

The change of direction did the trick:

"In April, 1814 a vein was discovered which had a good appearance ... After driving through the vein, which was 2 feet wide, a rise was made to the low flat of the great limestone, where the vein was nearly filled with carbonate of lead or white ore ... Thus commenced, at wages of nearly £10 per week, the working of those immense stores of wealth which raised the proprietors to opulence,

and have been a source of extensive employment to the labouring classes in Alston Moor ... The ease with which it has generally been worked is one of the great causes of its value, being entirely worked by the pick without the aid of blasting".

The efforts of the partnership and their outlay of a comparatively modest £360 were more than rewarded by the discovery of these very rich veins that were between ten and twelve feet in width. By 1821 the value of silver extracted from the lead was £8,400, the miners were paid the enormous sum of £10 per week and the partners made their fortunes. The clear profit was reckoned to be £30,000 per year, and it is worth repeating a newspaper report of 1888 which recalled that, *"when Hudgill Burn was at her best, more waste beer ran down the Nenthall sewer to the Nent, than is drunk in the whole parish now".*

The story as told gives the impression that John and Jacob were two ordinary lead miners, but in fact this was not the case. They were certainly the financiers of the enterprise but whether they ever wielded a pick at Hudgill is very doubtful. Research through church records revealed some of the background to the lives of the brothers.

John and Jacob Wilson moved to Alston Moor from West Allendale but their births, christenings and parentage cannot be found. John, the older brother, married Mary Bownas, known as Malley, in Allendale in 1790 and soon afterwards they moved to Nenthall where John became an innkeeper. Jacob, the younger brother, moved to Grassfield between Nenthead and Nenthall where he was a lead miner and he married Elizabeth Vipond in 1800.

The births of John's eight children were spread over twelve years from 1792 to 1804. For one entry in St. Augustine's Church records, in 1799, John's occupation was given as a miller but the next year he was again an innkeeper. For some time between 1800 and 1804 he moved with his family back to Ninebanks in Allendale, but by 1811 he was agent for the Grassfield and Brownley Hill mines.

Meanwhile at Grassfield, Jacob and Elizabeth began their family of six children in 1802, continuing to 1814. Jacob ceased to be a miner and became a merchant some time between 1805 and 1807.

John the innkeeper and Jacob the merchant must have been successful businessmen in order to accumulate enough capital to form a mining company. When their speculation paid off, the wealth produced by Hudgill Burn mine enabled the brothers to vastly improve their standards of living. John bought Nenthall and carried out alterations to give the building more or less its present appearance. Jacob bought Alston House at Townfoot in Alston. Between 1829 and 1834 John moved again, to Shotley Hall at Shotley Bridge near Consett.

By 1829 John and Jacob were classified as 'gentlemen' in the trades directory. In common with other mining companies, they rebuilt the school at Nenthall for the children of their employees. This was a mixed school endowed by the brothers, who *"contributed generously"* towards its upkeep, with places for eighty-four children.

The boom years of the Hudgill mine finished before 1834, but before then the brothers had had the sense to invest elsewhere, at Rotherhope Fell mine which also proved to be very productive.

By 1841 members of the Wilson families were distributed between Shotley Hall, Nenthall and Alston House. John died some time before this date and at Shotley Hall his widow, Mary, at eighty years old was living there with Mary Bownas, a great niece aged twenty and two male and two female servants. At Nenthall John's three youngest sons, Thomas aged forty-one, George aged thirty-nine and William aged thirty-seven were all of independent means and unmarried with two male and two female servants.

Meanwhile, at Alston House in 1841 Jacob, aged 70, was described as being of independent means, living with his wife Elizabeth, their daughter Sarah and grandchildren, Jacob Wilson aged four and granddaughter Elizabeth Fair aged three, with one male and one female servant.

Ten years later at Alston House, Jacob was eighty years old and he was a proprietor of land and mines. His wife Elizabeth was still alive and they had two female servants. Over at Shotley Hall in 1851 John's son Thomas was living there, having moved from Nenthall. He was still unmarried, his mother Mary had died some time before and he lived alone as a magistrate and was, like his uncle Jacob, a proprietor of land and lead and coal mines, with two male and three female servants. His brother George, now a lieutenant in the East India Company, married Grace Bowstead at Appleby in 1843 and in 1851, at the age of forty-nine, he was living at Nenthall with his wife and one male and one female servant.

Finally, Jacob Wilson died at Alston House on the 7th July 1858 at the advanced age of eighty-eight.

APPENDIX A

The Boundary of Alston Moor

The Boundary of Alston Moor was walked by Greenwich Hospital Commissioners in 1761, which is interesting to follow on a map, and it was confirmed as follows:-

"Beginning at the foot of Ayle Burn from thence to the head thereof, from thence to Willyshawrigg end, from thence to the top of Willyshaw Rigg, from thence in a direct line to Long Cleugh Hill, from thence in a direct line to Long Cross Pool, east of Long Cross, from thence to the foot of Mere Syke, from thence up the said syke to the head thereof, from thence in a direct line to Hardrigg end, from thence as the Heavens water divides to Blakelaws Cross, from thence as the Heavens water divides to High Raise, from thence (crossing the road leading from above Nentsbury) to Wellhope Head, from thence as the Heavens water divides to Dod End, from thence as Heavens water divides to Guddinghillhead, from thence as the water divides to the foot of the ditch at Ramsgill alias Redgroves Head, from thence along the said ditch to the end thereof, from thence as the water divides to Killhopehead, from thence along Killhope Head as the water divides to a place fifty yards east of Killhope Cross, where the said cross formerly stood it being removed some years ago as a mark for the convenience of travellers. From thence as the water divides to a place two hundred yards east of Shorts Cross where the said Cross formerly stood, it being likewise some time ago removed as a direction or guide for travellers, from thence as the water divides to the Nagshead from thence as the water divides to the road on Wellhope Edge, from thence as the water divides to Eedstones, from thence as the water divides to Penny Mea Hill, from thence up Penny Mea (Leaving the tarns a little on the right hand) to Burnhope Seat alias Scraithhead from whence as the water divides to a part of Scraithhead where the Bishop of Durham, Lord Darlington, and Greenwich Hospital Lordships join in a point from thence in a direct line to Crookburnhead, from thence down Crookburn to the foot

*thereof, where it joins Teeswater, from thence up the Tees to the head
thereof, from thence to the summit of Cross Fell, from thence as the
water divides to the north end of Cross Fell, from thence as the water
divides to Greyhound Stones, from thence in a direct line to
Cashburnhead or Well, from thence down Cashburn to the foot of
Cornrigg Burn, from thence down Cashburn, to the foot of Dirtpot
Burn, where the said Cashburn alters to the name of Shield Water,
alias Cashburn, to the foot of Swartbeck Burn where there stands a
fold called Swartbeck Fold, from thence down Shield Water alias
Cashburn to Snittergill Burn foot where the name alters to
Greencastle Water, alias Cashburn, from thence to Rowgillburn foot,
from thence up Rowgill Burn to Meerburn foot, from thence up
Meerburn to Dick Lees Cabin, from thence up the said burn to where
the burn divides, from thence up the westermost burn, called
Meerburn, to the Half Dyke, from thence to Parkinstones, or Old
Anthony's Chair, from thence to Parkinstones on the south of and near
Parkinson's Fold, from thence to Benty Hill Currock, from thence as
the water divides to Rowgillhead, from thence to the height of
Hartside, from thence to Colecleughhead, from thence to Little
Daffenside, from thence to Great Daffenside Currock, from thence to
Blackfell Currock, from thence to Thiefsykehead, as the water divides
to the head of Candlesievesyke, from thence in a direct line to Woogill
Tarn, from thence as the water divides to Smith's Stone, from thence
to Calflesshead, from thence down Woogill Burn to Gilderdale Burn,
from thence down the same to the foot thereof, and from thence up
the Tyne to Ayleburn foot where the boundary first began."*

APPENDIX B

Stories of Alston Moor

Surprisingly, Alston Moor does not abound with legends. There are authenticated stories such as that of the Garrigill poachers and several houses have their ghosts, which is par for the course in an old town, but actual legends are few.

A tunnel is supposed to pass from the farm of Corbygates near Alston, a distance of 1¾ miles as the crow flies north west to Randalholme, a fourteenth century tower house. While this is physically possible, there would have to be a very good reason for such an undertaking. If it exists, the tunnel must have been some sort of defensive measure. In mediaeval times Corbygates was a place of importance, a large settlement situated on the main road from Alston to Corbridge, while Randalholme was for centuries the residence of people of power and influence in the area. From this, connections can be inferred.

In reality, there is a curious tunnel that runs from near the Nent Force, towards and even under Alston, before rising vertically for some twenty feet and arriving at an abrupt halt. There is no reason to suppose it was for mining, so, what was its purpose?

The only good, fruity, traditional legends are around Garrigill.

In 1908 Caesar Caine related an old custom that Garrigill folk used to carry the coffins of the deceased three times around the church before departing for the grave, but offers no explanation.

Cross Fell apparently used to be known as Fiends Fell, and according to Caesar Caine, this was due to *"evil spirits which are said in former times to have haunted the summit of the hill, and continued their haunts and nocturnal vagaries upon it, until St. Austin, as it is said, erected a cross and an altar whereon he offered the Holy Eucharist by which he counter-charmed those hellish fiends and broke their haunts"*.

Part of Cross Fell is still called Fiends Fell, perhaps because the winds still howl up there in a devilish manner, but St. Austin (St. Augustine) in fact never went near the spot.

The remaining legend is that of the 'Corpse Road' from Garrigill over

Cross Fell to Kirkland. In this story it was supposed that there was a time when Garrigill did not have its own burial ground and there was an ecclesiastical connection with Kirkland parish in the Eden valley, and corpses are said to have been transported over Cross Fell for interment in Kirkland churchyard. There is no evidence to support this except for one story told to William Wallace which related to a time about the middle of the 17th century.

"A corpse was taken from Garrigill, in the depth of winter, to be interred at Kirkland. The funeral party was overtaken with a snowstorm, and had to return home to save their lives, leaving the coffin on the top of Cross Fell, where it remained for a fortnight. When the storm subsided they brought the corpse back to Garrigill and buried it in a piece of glebe land."

Certainly there was communication across the fell, as the bridleway called the Black Band Road testifies, and when the upper South Tyne was more populous, and the mines were in operation, it would have been a fairly busy route, since the Eden valley was a source of food and men might have come seeking work. But if Garrigill had ever been without a burial ground, it would have been before c.1200 and the deceased would have been buried in Alston.

The basis for the story told to Wallace could be that a resident of Kirkland, or someone who had been born in that parish, was visiting or staying in Garrigill and had died there, so it would be a natural desire on everyone's part to have the deceased buried in his or her native soil, hence the attempted journey across Cross Fell.

In the days when Shaw House on the Hartside Road was still a pub, a story tells how some miners on their way back to Alston late one evening, decided that they would like a free drink, so they played a trick. They quietly let the landlord's cattle out onto the road and led them a little distance away. Then, with a great deal of noise and fuss, drove them back to the pub again, waking the landlord. Believing, as the miners intended, that the cattle had got out by themselves and the miners were the saviours of the situation, the landlord gave them drinks all round.

At the High School, when Mr. Cox was the master, he was a bit too handy with the stick and the boys decided to teach him a lesson of their own. The boys drew straws and the boy with the shortest straw had to fill the front of his shirt with offal they had collected from the butcher's and then deliberately act up in front of Mr. Cox. Mr. Cox duly responded and hauled the boy out for a beating. At the first stroke the offal fell out onto the floor, Mr. Cox's face turned white and he nearly passed out. What happened afterwards is not known.

More recently a dramatic, tragic event happened within living memory. The Newcastle Journal told the story on Wednesday September 14th. 1949.

Charles Kennedy, a young man from Morpeth in Northumberland, hired a taxi in Stanhope, told the driver, Ernest Ingram, to go up to Stanhope Common, where Kennedy shot him and buried him under a pile of stones on the moors above Stanhope. Kennedy then drove to Alston, parked in the Market Square on the opposite side of the road to the bank and went into the bank carrying a brown brief case. A witness said that he appeared to be a commercial traveller.

There were only two people in the bank at the time - the manager, Mr. A.J.S. Steele, and his assistant, James Rush. Kennedy asked to see the manager and was shown into his private office.

Kennedy produced a revolver and demanded money. Steele resisted and during the struggle he was shot in the stomach and badly wounded, but he was able to touch the alarm bell. After firing the shot Kennedy dashed to the car without any cash and made his escape. He drove away down Front Street, narrowly missing several people, and then off towards Penrith. He got as far as Langwathby, twelve miles from Alston, when he realised that the police were closing in on him. Kennedy then shot himself. Mr. Steele died a few hours later.

In Mr. Steele's memory on 30th April 1950 four bells were installed by public subscription in St. Augustine's Church where he had been a churchwarden.

SOME REFERENCES AND FURTHER READING

Individual references for the innumerable pieces of information have not been listed because it would double the size of this book. Readers will have to take it on trust that each statement has its primary source or reputable secondary source.

(Note :- CWAAS refers to Cumberland and Westmorland Antiquarian and Archaeological Society Transactions. OS = Old Series; NS = New Series)

Armstrong Chester, A Pilgrimage from Nenthead

Barnes June C.F.; Radical Politics in Carlisle, 1790-1850; Thesis for Ph.D.; University of Lancaster; 1981

Caine C.; Capella de Gerardegile; 1908.

Clues J.A.; History of Alston Parish Church; privately published.

Cumbria County Council; Cumbria Coal Local Plan; Draft Written Statement for Consultation; 1988.

Daysh G.H.J. & Watson E.M.; Cumberland - An Industrial Survey; The Cumberland Development Council Ltd.; 1951

Edge B.; The History of Leadgate-in-Alston School; Brian Edge; 2009

Fair M.C.; An Interim review of types of Bronze Spear-heads and Axes of Cumberland, etc; CWAAS N.S. Vol.45; 1946.

Fairbairn R.A.; The Mines of Alston Moor; Published by R.A. Fairbairn; 2nd Edition, 2008.

Fairbairn R.A. & Robertson A.F.: The Iron Mines on and about Alston Moor; British Mining Memoirs No.69; 2001

Ferguson R.S.; Why Alston is in the Diocese of Durham, and in the County of Cumberland; CWAAS O.S. Vol.8; 1884.

Foster W.; A Treatise on a Section of the Strata from Newcastle-upon-Tyne to Cross Fell; 3rd Edn; 1883; reprinted Davis Books; 1985.

Gilbert T.; Observations upon the Orders and Resolutions of the House of Commons, with respect to the Poor, Vagrants, and Houses of Correction; 1775.

Graham T.H.B.; Alston; CWAAS N.S. Vol.31; 1930.

Greenwich Hospital Boundary Rolls; 1761, et. seq.

Hardy, J.; St. Augustine of Canterbury, Alston; A History of the Parish Church; 2007

Hunt C.J.; The Lead Miners of the Northern Pennines; Manchester

University Press; 1970.

Hunter T.; The Alston Foundry Story; privately printed; reference copy in Alston Library

Jackson E.; On a Bronze Tripod Vessel, found near Alston; CWAAS N.S. Vol.8; 1907.

Jarvis R.C.; The Jacobite Risings of 1715 and 1745; Cumberland County Council Record Series; Vol.1, 1954; Vol.2 1972.

Jenkins S.C.; The Alston Branch; Oakwood Press; 1991.

Maryon H.; Excavation of Two Bronze Age Barrows at Kirkhaugh Northumberland Arch. Aeliana Vol.13; 1936.

Mingay G.E.; Rural Life in Victorian England; William Heinemann Limited; 1976.

Monkhouse F.J.; Pre-Elizabethan Mining Law, with special reference to Alston Moor; CWAAS N.S. Vol.42; 1941.

Nall Rev. W.; Alston; CWAAS O.S. Vol.8; 1884.

Nanson W.; Notes on Alston Manorial Records; CWAAS O.S. Vol.8; 1884.

Nicholson J. & Burn R.; The History and Antiquities of Westmorland and Cumberland; Vol. 2; 1777.

Pearson, Joseph, (unpublished) diaries 1849-1856.

Penfold J.; The Clockmakers of Cumberland; Brampton Historical Society; 1976.

Ragg Rev. F.W.; Mauld's Meaburn, the Alston Mines, and a branch of the Veteriponts; CWAAS N.S. Vol.11; 1910.

Raistrick A.; Two Centuries of Industrial Welfare; Kelsall & Davis; 1988.

Robertson A.F.; Whitley Castle; A Roman Fort near Alston in Cumbria; Hundy Publications; 1996, 2007 Edn.

Robertson A.F.; Limekilns of the North Pennines; North Pennines Heritage Trust; 1999

Robertson A.F.; The Walton Family, A Lead Mining Dynasty of the northern Pennines; Hundy Publications; 2004

Robertson A.F.; Old News from Alston Moor (articles); Hundy Publications; 2007

Sopwith Thomas; An Account of the Mining District of Alston Moor, Weardale & Teesdale; 1833; Davis Books 1984.

Thomas Nicholas; Guide to Prehistoric England; Batsford/BCA; 1976 Edn.

Thompson William; A glance back to the 17th century life and customs; lecture at Alston; Cumberland News, 21st Dec. 1925.

Wallace William; Alston Moor; Its Pastoral People: Its Mines and Miners; 1890; Davis Books 1986.

Walton J.; The Mediaeval Mines of Alston; CWAAS N.S. Vol.45; 1946.

Welford R.; Alston Manor Paine Roll; Arch. Aeliana 3rd Ser. Vol.8; 1912.

Wilkinson P.; The Nentforce Level and Brewery Shaft; North Pennines Heritage Trust; 2001

Wilkinson P.; Old Alston; Stenlake Publishing; 2009

Williams L.A.; Road Transport in Cumbria in the 19th Century; George Allen & Unwin Ltd.; 1975.

Miscellaneous:-

Floods on the River Tyne & Tributaries 1699-1986; AMHS Archives.

Ordnance Survey; Place names on maps of Scotland and Wales; 1990.

Original documents, Trades Directories and Census Returns held in the County Records Office, Carlisle, the City Library, Carlisle, Church and Chapel registers and the Archives of Alston Moor Historical Society.

ACKNOWLEDGEMENTS

I would like to thank the many people have contributed to this book over the years by passing on information, giving leads for research, and especially by making documents and photographs available to the public by donating them to the Alston Moor Historical Society.